Communications in Computer and Information Science   1847

Rationale

The CCIS series is devoted to the publication of proceedings of computer science conferences. Its aim is to efficiently disseminate original research results in informatics in printed and electronic form. While the focus is on publication of peer-reviewed full papers presenting mature work, inclusion of reviewed short papers reporting on work in progress is welcome, too. Besides globally relevant meetings with internationally representative program committees guaranteeing a strict peer-reviewing and paper selection process, conferences run by societies or of high regional or national relevance are also considered for publication.

Topics

The topical scope of CCIS spans the entire spectrum of informatics ranging from foundational topics in the theory of computing to information and communications science and technology and a broad variety of interdisciplinary application fields.

Information for Volume Editors and Authors

Publication in CCIS is free of charge. No royalties are paid, however, we offer registered conference participants temporary free access to the online version of the conference proceedings on SpringerLink (http://link.springer.com) by means of an http referrer from the conference website and/or a number of complimentary printed copies, as specified in the official acceptance email of the event.

CCIS proceedings can be published in time for distribution at conferences or as post-proceedings, and delivered in the form of printed books and/or electronically as USBs and/or e-content licenses for accessing proceedings at SpringerLink. Furthermore, CCIS proceedings are included in the CCIS electronic book series hosted in the SpringerLink digital library at http://link.springer.com/bookseries/7899. Conferences publishing in CCIS are allowed to use Online Conference Service (OCS) for managing the whole proceedings lifecycle (from submission and reviewing to preparing for publication) free of charge.

Publication process

The language of publication is exclusively English. Authors publishing in CCIS have to sign the Springer CCIS copyright transfer form, however, they are free to use their material published in CCIS for substantially changed, more elaborate subsequent publications elsewhere. For the preparation of the camera-ready papers/files, authors have to strictly adhere to the Springer CCIS Authors' Instructions and are strongly encouraged to use the CCIS LaTeX style files or templates.

Abstracting/Indexing

CCIS is abstracted/indexed in DBLP, Google Scholar, EI-Compendex, Mathematical Reviews, SCImago, Scopus. CCIS volumes are also submitted for the inclusion in ISI Proceedings.

How to start

To start the evaluation of your proposal for inclusion in the CCIS series, please send an e-mail to ccis@springer.com.

Marco Aiello · Johanna Barzen ·
Schahram Dustdar · Frank Leymann
Editors

Service-Oriented Computing

17th Symposium and Summer School, SummerSOC 2023
Heraklion, Crete, Greece, June 25 – July 1, 2023
Revised Selected Papers

 Springer

Editors
Marco Aiello 🆔
University of Stuttgart
Stuttgart, Germany

Johanna Barzen 🆔
University of Stuttgart
Stuttgart, Germany

Schahram Dustdar 🆔
TU Wien
Vienna, Austria

Frank Leymann 🆔
University of Stuttgart
Stuttgart, Germany

ISSN 1865-0929   ISSN 1865-0937 (electronic)
Communications in Computer and Information Science
ISBN 978-3-031-45727-2   ISBN 978-3-031-45728-9 (eBook)
https://doi.org/10.1007/978-3-031-45728-9

This Springer imprint is published by the registered company Springer Nature Switzerland AG
The registered company address is: Gewerbestrasse 11, 6330 Cham, Switzerland

Paper in this product is recyclable.

Preface

The 17th advanced Summer School on Service-Oriented Computing (SummerSOC 2023) continued a successful series of summer schools that started in 2007. Summer-SOC regularly attracts world-class experts in Service Oriented Computing (SOC) to present state-of-the-art research during a week-long program organized in several thematic tracks: IoT, formal methods for SOC, Cloud Computing, Data Science, Advanced Manufacturing, Software Architecture, Digital Humanities, Quantum Computing, and emerging topics. The advanced summer school is regularly attended by top researchers from academia and industry as well as by PhD and graduate students.

During the SummerSOC symposium original research contributions in the areas mentioned above were presented. All accepted contributions were submitted in advance and were peer-reviewed in a single-blind review process. All papers were reviewed by three reviewers per paper. Based on the reviews the program chairs accepted or rejected contributions. Out of 27 submitted contributions, only 9 were accepted, with an acceptance rate of less than 34%. The contributions were extensively discussed after their presentation during a separate poster session. In addition to the reviewers' comments, the feedback from these discussions was folded into the final version published in this special issue.

The volume is structured into three parts focusing on (i) distributed systems, (ii) smart*, and (iii) mixed technologies, each providing three contributions. The first article in the section on distributed systems introduces a conceptual framework for understanding real-world AI planning domains; this contribution received the SummerSOC Best Paper Award 2023, sponsored by D-Visor. The next article proposes an architecture that bridges the gap by empowering machine learning development with service-oriented computing principles, followed by an article that demonstrates that the often-prohibitive costs of dictionary generation exhibited by earlier approaches can be avoided by simply using cache entries for content encoding based on shared dictionary compression for the web. The section on smart* provides contributions devoted to privacy in connected vehicles from the perspectives of drivers as well as car manufacturers, services in smart manufacturing with a focus on comparing automated reasoning techniques for composition and orchestration, and pool games in various information environments; this last contribution received the SummerSOC Young Researcher Award, sponsored by ServTech & ICSOC. The final section, on mixed technologies, provides first an article presenting an efficient 'multiples of' oracle as composable operations that help quantum software developers to reuse them when creating complex solutions, followed by a contribution focusing on orchestrating information governance workloads as stateful services using the Kubernetes operator framework. The final article of the last part provides insights on serverless data exchange within federations.

August 2023

Marco Aiello
Johanna Barzen
Schahram Dustdar
Frank Leymann

Organization

General Chairs

Marco Aiello   Universität Stuttgart, Germany
Schahram Dustdar   Technische Universität Wien, Austria
Frank Leymann   Universität Stuttgart, Germany

Organization Committee

Johanna Barzen   Universität Stuttgart, Germany
George Koutras   OpenIT, Greece
Themis Kutsuras   OpenIT, Greece

Steering Committee

Marco Aiello   Universität Stuttgart, Germany
Schahram Dustdar   Technische Universität Wien, Austria
Johanna Barzen   Universität Stuttgart, Germany
Christoph Gröger   Bosch, Germany
Frank Hentschel   Universität zu Köln, Germany
Willem-Jan van Heuvel   Eindhoven University of Technology,
                             The Netherlands
Rania Khalaf   Inari, USA
Alexander Lazovik   University of Groningen, The Netherlands
Frank Leymann   Universität Stuttgart, Germany
Andreas Liebing   StoneOne AG, Germany
Kostas Magoutis   University of Crete, Greece
Massimo Mecella   Sapienza University of Rome, Italy
Bernhard Mitschang   Universität Stuttgart, Germany
Guadalupe Ortiz Bellot   Universidad de Cádiz, Spain
Dimitris Plexousakis   University of Crete, Greece
Wolfgang Reisig   Humboldt-Universität, Germany
Jakka Sairamesh   CapsicoHealth Inc., USA
Sanjiva Weerawarana   WSO2, Sri Lanka
Guido Wirtz   Universität Bamberg, Germany

Program Committee

Marco Aiello	Universität Stuttgart, Germany
Johanna Barzen	Universität Stuttgart, Germany
Steffen Becker	Universität Stuttgart, Germany
Wolfgang Blochinger	Hochschule Reutlingen, Germany
Uwe Breitenbücher	Universität Stuttgart, Germany
Antonio Brogi	Università di Pisa, Italy
Giacomo Cabri	University of Modena and Reggio Emilia, Italy
Guiliano Casale	Imperial College London, UK
Christian Decker	Hochschule Reutlingen, Germany
Stefan Dessloch	TU Kaiserslautern, Germany
Schahram Dustdar	TU Wien, Austria
Sebastian Feld	TU Delft, The Netherlands
Melanie Herschel	Universität Stuttgart, Germany
Willem-Jan van Heuvel	Eindhoven University of Technology, The Netherlands
Dimka Karastoyanova	University of Groningen, The Netherlands
Christian Kohls	Technische Hochschule Köln, Germany
Ralf Küsters	Universität Stuttgart, Germany
Winfried Lamersdorf	Universität Hamburg, Germany
Alexander Lazovik	University of Groningen, The Netherlands
Frank Leymann	Universität Stuttgart, Germany
Kostas Magoutis	University of Crete, Greece
Massimo Mecella	Sapienza University of Rome, Italy
Bernhard Mitschang	Universität Stuttgart, Germany
Daniela Nicklas	Universität Bamberg, Germany
Guadalupe Ortiz Bellot	Universidad de Cádiz, Spain
Adrian Paschke	Freie Universität Berlin, Germany
Cesare Pautasso	University of Lugano, Switzerland
Srinath Perera	WSO2, Sri Lanka
Dimitris Plexousakis	University of Crete, Greece
René Reiners	Fraunhofer FIT, Germany
Wolfgang Reisig	Humboldt-Universität, Germany
Norbert Ritter	Universität Hamburg, Germany
Jakka Sairamesh	CapsicoHealth Inc., USA
Harald Schoening	Software AG, Germany
Ulf Schreier	Hochschule Furtwangen, Germany
Heiko Schuldt	Universität Basel, Switzerland
Stefan Schulte	TU Wien, Austria
Holger Schwarz	Universität Stuttgart, Germany
Stefan Tai	TU Berlin, Germany

Damian Tamburri	Eindhoven University of Technology, The Netherlands
Massimo Villari	Università degli Studi di Messina, Italy
Stefan Wagner	Universität Stuttgart, Germany
Sanjiva Weerawarana	WSO2, Sri Lanka
Guido Wirtz	Universität Bamberg, Germany
Uwe Zdun	Universität Wien, Austria
Alfred Zimmermann	Hochschule Reutlingen, Germany
Olaf Zimmermann	Hochschule für Technik Rapperswil, Switzerland

Additional Reviewers

Ghareeb Falazi
Nicolas Huber
Andrea Morichetta
Marie Salm
Mostafa Hadadian Nejad Yousefi

Contents

Distributed Systems

Understanding Real-World AI Planning Domains: A Conceptual Framework

Ebaa Alnazer$^{(\boxtimes)}$ and Ilche Georgievski

Service Computing Department, IAAS, University of Stuttgart, Germany,
Universitätsstrasse 38, 70569 Stuttgart, Germany
{ebaa.alnazer,ilche.georgievski}@iaas.uni-stuttgart.de

Abstract. Planning is a pivotal ability of any intelligent system being developed for real-world applications. AI planning is concerned with researching and developing planning systems that automatically compute plans that satisfy some user objective. Identifying and understanding the relevant and realistic aspects that characterise real-world application domains are crucial to the development of AI planning systems. This provides guidance to knowledge engineers and software engineers in the process of designing, identifying, and categorising resources required for the development process. To the best of our knowledge, such support does not exist. We address this research gap by developing a conceptual framework that identifies and categorises the aspects of real-world planning domains in varying levels of granularity. Our framework provides not only a common terminology but also a comprehensive overview of a broad range of planning aspects exemplified using the domain of sustainable buildings as a prominent application domain of AI planning. The framework has the potential to impact the design, development, and applicability of AI planning systems in real-world application domains.

Keywords: AI Planning · Real-World Planning Domains · Conceptual Framework

1 Introduction

Artificial Intelligence (AI) planning is the process of finding and organising a course of action to achieve some designated goals [20]. The field of AI planning has matured to such a degree that it is increasingly used to solve planning problems in real application domains, such as autonomous driving [5], intelligent buildings [18], robotics [36], and cloud computing [19]. In these application domains, various types of AI planning techniques have been used that differ in their assumptions and applicability for solving different planning problems. All the techniques, however, require gathering and formulating adequate and relevant knowledge of the application domain. This is in fact one of the phases needed to design and develop AI planning systems. Other phases include requirement analysis, selecting a suitable planning type, designing the planning systems, etc. [14].

M. Aiello et al. (Eds.): SummerSOC 2023, CCIS 1847, pp. 3–23, 2023.
https://doi.org/10.1007/978-3-031-45728-9_1

A crucial process that should precede the development of an operational and successful planning system is identifying and understanding relevant and realistic planning aspects that capture the complexity and characteristics of the application domain without making any simplified assumptions. This process is essential as it needs to guide all the phases of the development process of a planning system that can be utilised in actual settings. However, this process is difficult because AI planning covers a broad range of aspects considering the physics, functions, and qualities of the application domain. Despite all this, there are currently no mechanisms that can support software engineers and knowledge engineers in this process.

Our aim is, therefore, to conceptualise the *realism* of planning domains. To this end, we develop a top-down approach in which we explore and analyse the characteristics of planning domains in the existing literature. The outcome is a *conceptual framework* that contains realistic aspects of planning domains and corresponding categories with varying levels of granularity. The framework would form the basis of the design, identification, and categorisation of elements (e.g., planning domain models, planning software components or services, provenance data) for real-world planning applications. In particular, the benefits of the realistic-aspects framework can be summarised as follows.

- It helps to advance towards a common and inclusive notion of the realism of AI planning domain models.
- It serves as a basis for characterising planning problems based on their requirements. This offers useful guidelines for planning and software engineers through all the phases of planning system development on which methods and tools can reflect the requirements.
- It can drive the development of AI planning techniques and tools to address real-world planning problems' aspects.
- It provides means for comparing different AI planning systems based on their support of the real-domain aspects.
- It lays the groundwork for other AI planning research on the topics of improving the applicability of AI planning in real-world applications and guiding planning engineers in the development of planning systems.
- It highlights some aspects simplified in the existing literature on AI planning.

The rest of the paper is organised as follows. Section 2 provides the necessary fundamentals and the problem statement. Section 3 presents our methodology to develop the conceptual framework. Section 4 introduces our conceptual framework by focusing on the categories at the highest level of granularity. Finally, Sect. 5 concludes the paper with a discussion of our findings and future work.

2   Fundamentals and Problem Statement

We provide a brief introduction to AI planning followed by discussions on planning domain knowledge and designing AI planning systems, where we highlight the importance of having and understanding realistic aspects of planning domains. This serves as our basis to then state the problem our work focuses on.

2.1 Artificial Intelligence (AI) Planning

Artificial Intelligence (AI) planning is a subfield of AI that focuses on researching and developing planning systems that aim to find, organise and execute a course of action, i.e., a plan, in order to achieve some designated goal [20]. Depending on how complex and realistic the application domain is, one can employ various types of planning. The most basic but widely used type of planning is classical planning. It is based on the concept of actions and makes restrictive assumptions about how the environment of the application domain looks like. In particular, the environment is fully controllable, observable, deterministic, and static (no exogenous events), without temporal properties (actions are instantaneous), and plans are linearly ordered sequences of actions. Other planning types aim at relaxing some of these assumptions. Examples include probabilistic planning, which allows actions to have probabilistic effects, and temporal planning, which allows actions to have durations and considers the temporal interaction between them. Hierarchical Task Network (HTN) planning is another type of planning but one that breaks with the tradition of classical planning by introducing a hierarchy over actions with the help of tasks that can be refined into smaller subtasks using so-called decomposition methods that represent specific knowledge from the application domain [15].

2.2 Planning Domain Knowledge

AI planning is a knowledge-based technique, meaning, to compute plans, AI planning systems require relevant and adequate knowledge about the application domain. The knowledge consists of a *planning domain model* and an associated *problem instance*. A planning domain model is a formal representation of the domain knowledge, which is an abstract and conceptual description of the application domain. A problem instance is a specification of a particular planning scenario to be solved within this domain.

In classical planning, a planning domain model formalises the domain knowledge in terms of domain objects with their relations and properties, and *actions* that can change the state of the environment. A problem instance is specified via an initial state and set of goal states that need to be reached. The planning domain models and problem instances used by other types of planning support more constructs, thus enabling the expression of more complex and realistic domain knowledge. For example, in HTN planning, the planning domain model is formalised in terms of actions, *compound tasks*, and *methods*. Actions are defined the same as in classical planning. Compound tasks are more complex tasks than actions and need to be refined into smaller tasks utilising methods. Methods enable encoding of how compound tasks can be achieved by achieving smaller tasks through the means of specific domain knowledge.

2.3 Designing AI Planning Systems

The design and development of a typical AI planning system can go through various phases [14]. In the first phase, relevant requirements should be analysed.

The requirements can be functional, non-functional, user-related, and domain-oriented. Having relevant and well-defined requirements is of utmost importance as it affects the suitability of the intended planning system to address the *real-world aspects* of the application domain. So, this phase is crucial as it provides the ingredients necessary to select a suitable planning type, design a planning domain model, design the system architecture, and define relevant provenance data. The main concern of the second phase is the selection of a suitable planning type. The selection depends on the assumptions about how *realistic* the environment is (see Sect. 2.1). In the third phase, the requirements are used to formulate planning domain knowledge out of which a planning domain model is created. The proper execution of this phase in terms of detailed knowledge encoding and management is essential as the lack of relevant or ill-described knowledge can lead to planning domain models that do not reflect the *intended* aspects of the corresponding application domain [33]. This can lead, eventually, to unsatisfactory plans that cannot be executed in real settings [34]. In the fourth phase, the planning system is designed, where the choice of relevant software-engineering principles, design approaches and patterns, and other specific techniques is dictated by the type and nature of the output of the previous three phases. For example, if we want to develop a planning system for any planning domain, e.g., sustainable buildings, that computes plans, schedules, and executes the plan actions in real-time, then we need to *adequately* structure and connect *relevant* planning components.

2.4   Problem Statement

Understanding and gathering the relevant aspects characterising real-world planning problems is crucial to the design, development, and applicability of AI planning systems. In particular, this should precede all development phases of AI planning systems since these relevant aspects should be considered and reflected during the execution of each development phase. The way these aspects are reflected depends on the particularities of each phase. For example, in the third phase, where planning engineers create a domain model out of the planning knowledge they acquired, it is necessary to see how the different aspects are reflected in the planning constructs used in the model. Similarly, in phase 5, when selecting suitable AI planning tools, planning engineers should have adequate knowledge about the aspects that the planning system should support to be able to select the tools that support these aspects. There exist some works that focus on providing means to support the design of planning domain knowledge. These works assume that relevant requirements and specifications of relevant domain knowledge are already given by stakeholders or domain experts. The aim of knowledge engineers is to satisfy these requirements and specifications in their design of planning domain knowledge. Usually, the process of designing this knowledge is done in an ad-hoc manner, and the quality of the resulting planning domain models depends mainly on the skills of the knowledge engineers and, if available, the tools they use [27, 31]. In this context, a quality framework is suggested aiming at developing systematic processes that support a more comprehensive notion of planning domain quality [31]. Some other studies focus on conceptualising planning functionalities as distinct software components so that they can be directly and flexibly used to address the intended requirements of application domains (e.g., [13]).

However, to the best of our knowledge, there is currently no support for software engineers and knowledge engineers in the process of identifying relevant and realistic aspects of real-world planning domains necessary for the development of essential planning elements (i.e., requirements, planning types, planning domain models, planning system design). Our work is positioned within this research gap and aims at answering the following research question: *What are the realistic aspects that should be considered in the process of developing AI planning systems for real-world domains and how those aspects can be meaningfully organised?*

3 Approach

To address our research question, we perform top-down exploratory research on existing literature to find relevant information related to the realism of planning domains and create the conceptual framework of realistic aspects for planning domains. We illustrate the elements of the conceptual framework using the domain of *Sustainable Buildings*, which is one prominent example of real-world application domains.

3.1 Methodology

Our methodology is illustrated in Fig. 1. The first step is to identify the literature from which we can obtain initial ideas about realistic aspects of planning domains as discussed in the literature. We start with literature known to us and then use relevant terms to search for and explore other relevant studies. We are interested in studies that analyse the requirements and characteristics of application domains (e.g., building automation, smart homes, ubiquitous computing) by following a systematic way and/or developing a framework. Another type of research we are interested in focuses on characteristics that exist in real-world planning domains generally, i.e., not in a specific domain. A third strand of research that we explore focuses on providing quality measures to assess the quality of planning knowledge or that discuss what aspects can define the usefulness of the domains. The last strand of research that interests us contains some works that provide a systematic process of knowledge engineering and modelling of AI planning domains. The output of **Step 1** is 20 identified studies.

We use the set of identified studies to extract statements about realism in planning domains, and then identify and gather realistic aspects as described in these studies (**Step 2**). The output of this step is a collection of realistic characteristics. After that, we follow a descriptive research method to depict, describe, and organise the collected aspects [21,35]. Thus, in **Step 3**, we categorise the gathered aspects based on their relevance to one another. We also refine the

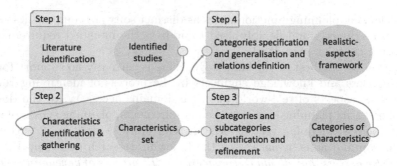

Fig. 1. Our methodology for defining the realistic-aspects framework. Rectangles represent the steps, circles represent the output of each step, and arrows illustrate that the output of each step represents the input of the following one.

gathered information of each category by combining similar aspects and distinguishing different concerns. In this step, each category is annotated with a common feature that describes all the aspects within the category. Additionally, in this step, we further extract subcategories as defined in the corresponding identified studies. The output of **Step 3** is a collection of identified categories and subcategories. Lastly, in **Step 4**, we identify the different relations between the categories, subcategories, and aspects. We organise these as a hierarchy of aspects and their categories with varying degrees of granularity. The final outcome of our approach is a conceptual framework represented by the hierarchy. We call this framework the *realistic-aspects framework*.

3.2   Running Example: Sustainable Buildings Domain

Sustainable buildings are smart buildings whose operation depends on the effectiveness and efficiency of their Building Management Systems (BMSs). These are computer-and-device-based control systems concerned with monitoring, storing, and communicating data, in addition to supervising, controlling, and automating the various systems in buildings [26]. Examples of devices in sustainable buildings include sensors (e.g., position and temperature sensors), and actuators (e.g., switches on ceiling lamps). Systems in sustainable buildings can include Heating, Ventilation, Air conditioning (HVAC), lighting, access control, security, electrical, and other interrelated systems. The main objectives of BMSs include increasing safety, improving people's productivity, cutting energy consumption; hence preserving finite resources, using non-carbon sources when possible to lower the CO_2 footprint, and lowering the costs of consumers and businesses while preserving users' comfort [10,18]. This is especially true for buildings that are connected to a smart grid, which makes it possible to include renewable sources and provides dynamic pricing and energy offers coming from competing providers [12]. The advent of the Internet of Things (IoT) and advances in AI offer significant opportunities to improve the limited control capabilities offered by current building management systems, such as the reactive control and feedback mechanisms [17,18].

4   The Framework

We gather and extract realistic aspects of planning domains from the identified relevant studies. We categorise these realistic aspects into seven main categories based on their relevance to each other, namely: Objectives, Tasks, Quantities, Determinism, Agents, Constraints, and Qualities. We provide details on identified aspects and categories per study in Appendix 5.[1]

We use the identified aspects and categories to develop a conceptual framework in the form of a hierarchy of realistic aspects for planning domains. Figures 2 and 3 show the realistic-aspects framework. We split the hierarchy into two figures for better readability. The categories that we identified in **Step 3** form the highest level of the hierarchy. In the following, we organise the discussion of the realistic-aspects framework per category at the highest level.

4.1   Objectives

The first high-level category is related to the *Objectives* of planning domains. We categorise the Objectives based on their *Types* and *Granularity*. For the first category, we distinguish two types of goals as suggested in [16]. The first is *Soft Goals* or *Preferences*, which represent the non-mandatory user's desires that should be considered when solving planning problems in the domain. Considering our running example domain, the BMS might have the soft goal of keeping the offices in a building clean. The second is *Hard goals* or *Requests*, which, unlike the Preferences, define a mandatory behaviour of the planning system according to which planning problems in the domain should be solved. A hard goal in the Sustainable Buildings domain could be to maintain the energy consumption in the building under a certain threshold.

We further classify the goals into *Qualitative* and *Quantitative* goals. That is, in some domains, it might be required to express goals in terms of qualities that the system should meet, such as improving the comfort of the building occupants, or in terms of exact quantities that should be maintained or reached, such as minimising the operation costs of the building to a certain value per year. Additionally, goals, whether they are soft or hard, can be of an *Optimisation* nature or *Satisfaction* nature. In the first case, the goal is to find an optimal solution to the planning problem. For example, in the Sustainable Buildings domain, according to the market prices, the amount of stored energy, and the weather forecast, the goal could be to find an optimal plan that minimises the energy consumption of the building. In the second case, the goal is to satisfy the domain goal to a certain degree. For example, given the aforementioned

---

[1] Note that the categories and subcategories included in the table are the ones identified directly from the studies before any refinement and/or generalisation.

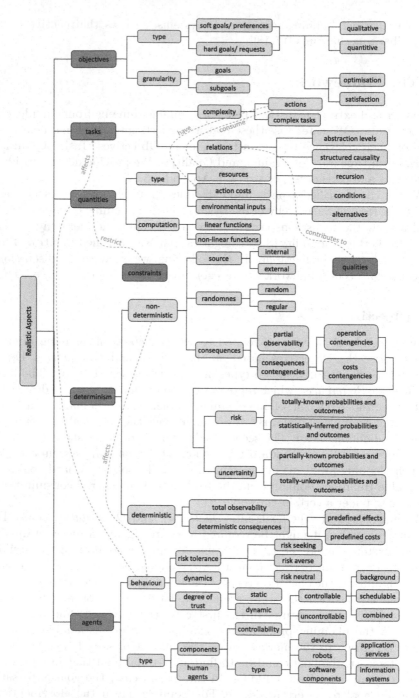

Fig. 2. Realistic-Aspects Framework (Part One). Rectangles represent the aspects, blue rectangles are the aspects of the highest level, and dashed arrows define the relationships between the aspects. (Color figure online)

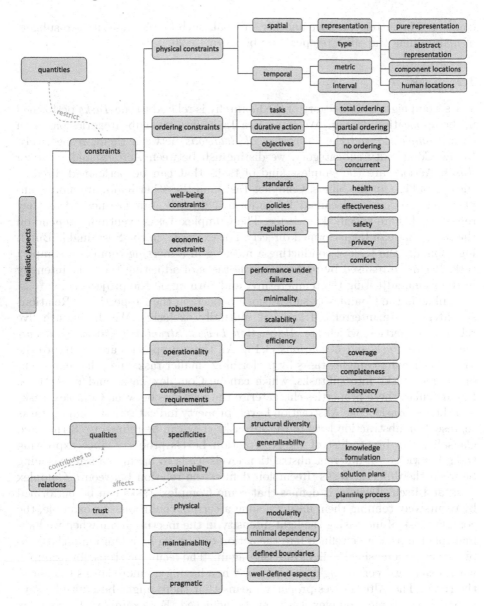

Fig. 3. Realistic-Aspects Framework (Part Two).

building conditions, the goal could be to compute plans that do not exceed a certain threshold of energy consumption.

For Granularity, in some application domains, we might need to express *Subgoals* of bigger goals. For example, the goal of maintaining cleanness in the offices could be a subgoal of a more coarse-grained goal of increasing occupants' comfort. The latter can have another subgoal, such as the quantitative subgoal of maintaining the office temperature between 15–20°.

4.2 Tasks

The second high-level category of the hierarchy is related to the *Tasks* performed in the application domain. We categorise Tasks into two subcategories based on their *Complexity* and the *Properties of Relations* between them, respectively. In the Complexity subcategory, we distinguish between *Actions* and *Complex Tasks*. Actions are the simplest kind of tasks that can be performed directly, such as pulling up the blinds. Complex Tasks, on the other hand, are more complex than Actions and cannot be performed directly, but are needed as they represent domain-specific knowledge. The Complex Tasks eventually depend on the tasks that can be performed directly. For example, in the Sustainable Buildings domain, the task of conducting a meeting in a meeting room is a complex task. It can be realised by performing the tasks of adjusting the light intensity in the room, adjusting the temperature, and turning on the projector.

Unlike in the Complexity subcategory, aspects in the Properties of Relations subcategory are interrelated and not mutually exclusive. We distinguish five relation properties, which are *Abstraction Levels, Structured Causality, Recursion, Alternatives*, and *Conditions* [3,18]. All these properties are related to the idea of achieving complex tasks by performing smaller tasks, i.e., the refinement of complex tasks into subtasks, which can be Complex Tasks and/or Actions. In particular, these properties characterise the relations between Complex Tasks and their subtasks. The Abstraction Levels property indicates that complex tasks represent an abstraction level to the subtasks they can be refined to. Structured Causality is a by-product of the Abstraction Levels property since expressing tasks knowledge in different abstraction levels leads to having causal reasoning between the different tasks. Recursion defines the relation between a Complex Task and itself. That is, it defines that some Complex Tasks can be performed by recursively refining them until reaching a certain condition. For example, the complex task of increasing the light intensity in the meeting room when we have multiple lamps can be refined into the action of turning on a lamp and the complex task of increasing the light intensity again. The recursion stops, for example, when reaching a certain light intensity or when having no more lamps to light in the room. The Alternatives property means that there might be multiple ways in which the same Complex Task can be achieved. For example, the complex task of increasing the light intensity can be performed by refining it to the task of pulling up the blinds or by refining it to the alternative task of turning on lamps. Finally, the Conditions property represents the situation where refining a Complex Task in a certain way has conditions that should be satisfied. For example, turning on lamps to increase the light intensity can only be done if there is not enough light coming from windows, i.e., if pulling up the blinds does not increase the light intensity to the required intensity level.

4.3 Quantities

The third high-level category of the hierarchy is related to *Quantities*. We categorise Quantities in planning domains based on their *Type* and how they should be computed. We call the latter subcategory *Computation*. In the first case, we distinguish three types of quantities; *Resources*, *Action costs*, and *Environmental Inputs*. Resources are quantities that define a bound to the allowed or possible consumption. They can be, for instance, money, fuel, energy, and time. In the Sustainable Buildings domain, the budget dedicated to the building operation represents a resource. Action costs represent the resource consumption incurred by performing actions. For example, if we consider the energy that is stored locally in the building as a resource, the action of turning on the heating system using locally stored energy results in a cost that equals the amount of consumed energy. The Environmental Inputs represent all measurable characteristics of the planning domain environment and the tasks performed in the domain. Examples of environmental inputs in the Sustainable Buildings domain include indoor temperature, CO_2 level, humidity, light intensity, energy demand, and battery capacity [17]. Similarly, drivers' trust in the autonomous vehicle is considered an environmental input [5]. We compute quantities based on the real-world concepts they express, where either *Linear* or *Non-linear functions* should be used [17]. For example, calculating temperature, battery charging, and tariff change requires using non-linear functions.

4.4 Determinism

The fourth high-level category of the hierarchy is related to whether the planning domain is deterministic or not. When the application domain is *Deterministic*, all conditions of the environment are *Totally observable* at all times. Additionally, in deterministic environments, actions work exactly as expected, i.e., they have *Predefined Consequences* and *Predefined Costs*. For example, in the Sustainable Buildings domain, if the heating system is 100% reliable, the action of turning it on will always lead to the heating system being turned on. Furthermore, if the energy prices are known with 100% certainty, the operation cost of the heating system, i.e., the cost of the action is predefined with certainty.

Most real-world planning domains are, however, *Non-deterministic* [4]. We categorise the non-determinism of planning domains based on the *Source*, *Randomness*, and *Consequences* of non-determinism. Sources might be *Internal*, meaning, they are related to the performer of the actions. These include, for example, internal malfunctions, and unreliability or limited capabilities of the agents. Sources might otherwise be *External*, i.e., related to environmental conditions that are external to the agent, such as the non-determinism of the weather conditions. The Randomness subcategory defines whether the non-determinism source is *Regular*, i.e., changes all the time, such as weather conditions, energy demand and market prices [10,11], or it is totally *Random*, such as a malfunction in the battery storage. The Consequences category defines the effects that the non-determinism sources have on the planning domain. The first type of consequences is related to *Partial Observability* of the surrounding environment. For example, an internal malfunction in the sensors responsible for detecting whether the person is working on his/her PC can lead to partial knowledge about the current conditions of the environment. The second type of Consequences is related to *Action Contingencies*, i.e., actions not working as expected [25]. These can be *Effect Contingencies* and/or *Cost Contingencies*, which means that actions do not have predefined effects on the environment and do not consume resources as expected, respectively. For example, turning on the radiator to heat the office might lead to the radiator not being turned on due to internal malfunction. Additionally, turning on the radiator might have costs that are hard to predefine with certainty. The reason for this could be not having enough locally stored energy due to unexpected weather conditions. This necessitates buying energy, which incurs costs that depend on the market prices.

With the existence of non-determinism in the environment, we can have a full spectrum of the degree of knowledge that is available about the *Action Consequences*. We might have *Full Knowledge* about the probability distribution and outcomes of actions or we might be able to *Statically infer* them. In both cases, we have *Risk* involved in the domain. We might, however, have only *Partial* or even *No Knowledge* about the probability distribution of the action outcomes. In these cases, we have *Uncertainty* in the domain. For the distinction between *Risk* and *Uncertainty* in AI planning, see [4].

4.5 Agents

The fifth high-level category is related to *Agents*, which are the performers of actions. We classify agents based on their *Type* and *Behaviour*. For the Type, we distinguish between *Human Agents* (e.g., occupants of the building) and non-human agents, which we refer to as *Components*. Components are further categorised based on their *Type* and *Controllability*. Types of components include *Devices* (e.g., actuators and batteries to store energy), *Robots* (e.g., teleconferencing and cleaning robots), or *Software Components*. The latter represents either *Application Services* that can be commercial (e.g., Microsoft PowerPoint) or have a specific purpose (e.g., application services to control the desired thresholds of lighting and heating), or *Information Systems* (e.g., platforms used to analyse smart building data and display them in a dashboard for monitoring) [16].

Regarding Controllability, Components in planning domains can be either *Controllable* or *Uncontrollable* [17]. Controllable components can be controlled directly and are mostly internal to the application domain. These include components that run in the *Background* all the time (e.g., water heating in buildings), *Schedulable Components* (e.g., dishwashers), or *Combined* components that can run in the background and be scheduled (e.g., space heating in buildings). On the other hand, Uncontrollable components are components whose operations cannot be controlled directly but depend mainly on conditions external to the application domain. An example of uncontrollable components in smart buildings is solar panels whose operations depend on weather conditions.

When dealing with domains that involve risk and uncertainty, the domain knowledge should reflect the *Behaviour* of the agents. That is, when risk and uncertainty exist in the domain, agents can have different preferences on how to make decisions during planning. These preferences are related to the agents' *Risk Tolerance* and the *Degree of Trust* they have in the planning system to make the right choices. We classify the agent's risk tolerance based on its *Degree* and *Dynamics*. For the Degree, we distinguish three risk tolerance degrees, namely *Risk-seeking*, *Risk-averse*, and *Risk-neutral*. For example, let us assume that a risk-seeking agent is confronted with two choices that have the same expected value of the outcomes. The first choice has a 100% probability of its outcome, i.e., it has a guaranteed outcome. However, although the second choice has the same expected value of outcomes, the probability of having a good outcome is very low. In this case, the risk-seeking agent will take risks and choose the second option hoping to end up with a good outcome. On the other hand, a risk-averse agent will avoid taking risks and prefer the first choice as it is guaranteed. A risk-neutral agent will only consider the expected value of the outcomes and thus will be indifferent to the risk involved in each option, i.e., it will be indifferent to the two options. Considering our running example, the building can get its electricity from two different sources; either from stored electricity generated locally by renewable resources or from electric utilities with varying prices and energy offers. The choice of whether to consume locally generated electricity or to purchase it from outside sources should be made under uncertainty about the future market prices and the future weather forecast. Let us assume that the building management system has the following information: there is a high probability of having a cloudy next day, i.e., no energy can be stored in the batteries and a small probability of having a sunny day. However, there is information about the day-ahead prices offered by different providers. The building management system might follow a risk-seeking attitude and decides not to purchase energy and rely on the small probability of having a sunny day, i.e., using solar energy.

Regarding the Dynamics of the agent's risk tolerance, the agent might have *Static* or *Dynamic* risk tolerance. Static risk tolerance means that the agent will have the same degree of risk tolerance in one-shot planning with the same domain conditions. On the other hand, Dynamic risk tolerance changes during the one-shot planning based on some factors, such as the resource amount remaining in the domain. For example, the BMS might be making all choices during planning based on risk-seeking tolerance, but once the locally stored energy goes under a certain threshold, it will become less risk tolerant.

4.6 Constrains

The sixth high-level category is about the *Constraints* in the application domain. We distinguish four different classes of constraints: *Physical Constraints*, *Ordering Constraints*, *Well-being Constraints*, and *Economic Constraints*. Physical Constraints relate agents and the actions they perform to each other with respect to space (i.e., *Spatial Constraints*) and time (i.e., *Temporal Constraints*). For example, a spatial constraint on the action of an occupant moving from the corridor to the office defines that the agent should be in the corridor before moving and will be in the office after performing the action. Another example where the agent is a component is a spatial constraint on the actions of the actuator that controls the blinds. That is, for the actuator to open the blinds, the actuator should be attached to the blinds. Spatial Constraints can be represented either abstractly or purely [2]. An abstract representation is a representation without considering any geometrical or physical laws, where actions are considered to be, for example, instantaneous. An example of this is assuming that an occupant's movement from the corridor to the office or the battery storing the energy generated from solar panels happens instantaneously. On the other hand, a pure representation considers the geometrical or physical laws and sometimes the spatiotemporal properties [6]. This means that representing the movement of an occupant requires considering the time needed for the movement and the spatial arrangement of the building, i.e., the locations of the corridor and the office. According to this, we categorise the Spatial Constraints based on the agents performing the spatially constrained actions into *Human Locations* and *Component Locations*. We also categorise them based on their representation into *Abstract Representation* and *Pure Representation*.

Similar to Spatial Constraints, Temporal Constraints might be defined with respect to the actions executed by agents and the relations between these actions. We distinguish two categories of Temporal Constraints *Metric Constraints* and *Interval Constraints*. The first type defines an absolute time point at which an action should be performed. For example, actions that turn off the lights in the whole building should be performed at the end of the working day. This type of constraints can also restrict the relations between different actions with respect to absolute time points. For example, we might have a constraint that restricts the action of opening the blinds in the room and turning on the room lights at the same time since this might lead to a waste of energy. Interval Constraints restrict the start and end time of actions. We refer to these actions as *Durative Actions*. In other words, they are defined on the time interval in which actions are performed. For example, there might be a temporal constraint that restricts when the cleaning robot can start and end cleaning in the office to avoid disturbing office occupants. Additionally, Temporal Constraints can restrict the relations between durative actions with respect to time. For example, there might exist a temporal constraint that requires the start of the air conditioner operation using locally stored energy to follow the end of the storing energy in batteries operation. Spatial and Temporal Constraints can also restrict the existence of agents with one another even if these agents are not performing actions. For example, in a health-sensitive situation, regulations might be in place that restrict the existence of more than a certain number of people in the same location (spatial constraint) at the same time (temporal constraint).

The second class of constraints is related to the *Ordering* between Objectives, Complex Tasks, or Durative Actions. These can have a *Strict Total Ordering*,

Partial Ordering, Require Concurrency, or can be *Unordered*. Ordering between objectives can represent the importance of these objectives. For example, the objective of maintaining occupants' safety cannot be compromised by satisfying other objectives, such as improving the occupants' comfort. In the context of objectives, concurrency ordering means that objectives have the same exact importance. For Durative Actions, we can have, for example, a strict ordering between the operation of storing energy and the operation of operating the air conditioner, or we can have a flexible order, i.e., unordered constraints, as long as the battery has enough energy. We can also have a partial order between durative actions, where we define a certain degree of order among them, i.e., some actions have a specific order of execution while others do not. This also applies to complex tasks.

The third class of constraints is called *Well-being Constraints*. These constraints are derived from regulations, policies, or standards of the application domain and aim at improving users' comfort, privacy, health, safety, and effectiveness [18]. For example, turning lights on/off and controlling their intensity in the office can follow some standards for lighting in indoor workplaces [18]. The fourth class of constraints is defined on the actions performed in the application domain and is of economical nature. Thus, we call it *Economical Constraints*. An example of these kinds of constraints can be a constraint on the maximum energy consumption, i.e., cost induced as a result of performing a specific operation.

The classes of constraints are not mutually exclusive. Well-being constraints, for example, can restrict the existence of multiple people in the same location, the existence of certain components with human beings at the same location, or the existence of people and/or components at the same time [17].

4.7   Qualities

The last high-level category of the framework is concerned with the *Qualities* of the different aspects of a planning domain and the overall planning system. Identifying the required qualities of the planning system, including all its elements, contributes directly to our goal of providing support to knowledge engineers and software engineers in the process of designing and developing the planning system.

We categorise the Qualities into eight classes. The first class is the *Robustness* class, which reflects how robust planning is to changes. This includes the domain's (1) *Minimality*, (2) *Scalability*, (3) *Efficiency*, and (4) *Performance under Failures*. These define (1) how compact is the model of the domain, such that the domain knowledge is modelled efficiently and there are no additional or unnecessary constructs; (2) how well the planning system enables solving planning problems of increased complexity; (3) how efficiently planning problems in this domain can be solved; and (4) how robust the planning system is against failures in some parts of it, respectively. These aspects characterise the planning system as a whole, but at the same time, are affected by the planning domain itself. For example, the efficiency quality depends partially on the planning system, but the domain structure, minimality, and encoding language may have a great impact on the efficiency of the planning system.

The second class is related to the compliance of the planning system and its elements with the requirements of the application domain. We call this class *Compliance with Requirements* and it includes: (1) *Coverage*, (2) *Completeness*, (3) *Accuracy*, and (4) *Adequacy*. Coverage defines to what extent the planning domain model covers all required aspects of the application area. Completeness means that the domain model enables the generation of all (and only) solution plans that are correct with respect to the domain specifications. Accuracy ensures that the domain model is a valid representation of the domain specifications, meaning it encodes all the aspects that are correct and relevant for the application domain. Adequacy is related to the expressive power of the planning modelling language to represent the requirements within a planning domain model in sufficient detail so that a complete planning domain model can be expressed. For more details and formal definitions of Completeness, Accuracy, and Adequacy aspects, see [27,30].

The third class is related to the *Specificities* of the application domain. This class includes *Structural diversity* and *Generalisability*. These are related to how well the planning domain model reflects the specificities of the application domain [3] and how easy it is to be generalised to enable solving planning problems with fewer or more specificities, respectively. For example, in the Sustainable Building domain, specificities of the domain include the task of preparing the meeting room. This task is specific to this domain. Generalisability in this domain can be achieved, for example, by having different abstraction levels of tasks (see Sect. 4.2).

The fourth class is related to the *Maintainability* of the planning system in general and the planning domain in particular. This class defines how easily the planning domain model can be modified to handle new requirements and includes (1) *Modularity*, (2) *Scope/Defined Boundaries*, (3) *Well-defined Aspects*, and (4) *Minimal Dependency*. Modularity is achieved when the planning system/domain model has clearly divided modules, thus, it is easier to modify a specific module without the need to change the whole planning system/domain model. This is also related to the planning system/planning domain model being scoped, i.e., having well-defined boundaries and aspects that precisely reflect the specific requirements of the application domain. Lastly, the fewer dependencies between the different modules in the planning system/domain model, the easier it is to be maintained.

The fifth class is related to the *Explainability* of the planning system behaviour and the planning knowledge, especially to non-experts. This is related to the (1) formation of the domain knowledge, (2) the formation of the plans computed in the domain, and (3) the planning process itself [5]. For example, the structured causality between tasks in the domain enables causal reasoning, which makes it easy to track and explain the behaviour of the system.

The last three classes are related to *Physical*, *Pragmatic* [31], and *Operationality* aspects [27,31]. The Physical class focuses on maximising the availability and accessibility of the planning domain models to interpreters to make sense of and revisit domain models. This class aims at maximising the availability of planning knowledge models such that future validations and evaluations can be performed. The Pragmatic class is related to the analysis of domain models after the design phase and focuses on how the changes made to domain models, as a result of using them in planning systems, can lead to the discovery of missing requirements. Operationality is related to the ability of planning systems to reason upon domain models and generate solution plans using bounded computational resources (e.g., memory usage). It focuses mainly on the quality and shape of the resulting plans and the speed of plan generation. For more details and formal definitions of the Physical, Pragmatic, and Operationality aspects, see [27,31].

5   Conclusions and Future Work

Despite the research advancements in AI planning, applying AI planning systems to solve real-world planning problems seems to be still challenging. Improving this situation requires understanding and considering the aspects that characterise real-world planning domains in all development phases of planning systems. In particular, knowledge engineers and software engineers should be supported in making informed choices when reasoning about relevant and realistic aspects of application domains that must be considered when developing planning systems. Currently, this process is not supported. The main obstacles seem to be the broad range of aspects of planning domains and the lack of unified notions of what makes a planning domain realistic.

We took a step forward in this direction by introducing a framework that conceptualises the notion of planning domains' realism. We gathered and analysed information about planning domains from existing literature and, consequently, developed a framework that categorises a large number of realistic aspects in multi-level granularity. The framework provides a common notion of planning domains' realism, highlights some aspects (e.g., uncertainty and risk) that are simplified and/or neglected in the literature of AI planning, can drive the development of service-oriented AI planning systems, and offers means for comparing different planning systems. For future work, we plan to synthesise metrics that can quantitatively evaluate the realism of planning domains and empirically verify and validate the conceptual framework on realistic application domains. We also want to explore the framework's usability for the design of service-oriented AI planning systems.

Appendix

Table 1 shows the identified studies, identified aspects in each study, subcategories as defined in the identified studies, and the category to which each aspect and subcategory belongs, respectively.

Table 1. Realistic aspects of planning domains in literature with the identified categories and subcategories.

Studies	Characteristics	Subcategories	Category
[16]	preferences	-	behavioural inputs
	Requests		
	device operations	-	behavioural outputs
	human operations		
	robot operations		
	application operations		
	information operations		
	(s) object and human locations	(s)patial, (t)emporal	physical properties
	(t) time points (metric constraints) and qualitative relations (intervals)		
	unexpected events	-	Uncertainty
	partial observability		
	operations contingencies		
[30]	definition of goals and subgoals	-	-
	accuracy	-	-
	adequacy	-	-
[24, 25]	definition of goals and subgoals	-	-
	expressing temporal constructs in goals	-	-
[23]	structural diversity	-	-
[28]	objects, relations, properties, and constraints	-	static knowledge
	object behaviour	-	dynamic knowledge
[4]	risk	-	-
	uncertainty	-	-
	risk attitude	-	-
[5]	trust	-	-
[3]	structural diversity	-	-
	action costs	-	-
	alternatives	-	-
[32]	explainability	-	-
[8]	efficiency	-	-
[22]	action costs	-	-
[17]	ambient operations	-	building operations
	electrical equipment operations		
	green operations		
	(c) background, schedulable, and combined	(c)ontrollable, (u)ncontrollable	building properties
	linear	-	quantities
	non-linear		
	well-being constraints	-	constraints
	operation constraints		
	temporal: required concurrency		
	ordering constraints		
	business constraints		
	strict-total ordering	-	objectives

(*continued*)

Table 1. (*continued*)

Studies	Characteristics	Subcategories	Category
[18]	occupant activity	-	-
	building properties	-	-
	activity area	-	-
	building condition	-	-
	social and economic (resource management)	-	quality conditions
	modularity/abstraction	-	-
	structured causality	-	-
	ordering control	-	-
	recursion	-	-
[1]	explainability	-	user-related requirements
	improvement of sustainability		
	safety		
	privacy		
	keeping the effectiveness of people		
	comfort		
	ordering constraints	-	-
	business, administrative, user, and system requirements	-	-
	minimize operation costs and environmental impact, and satisfy the power needs	-	objectives
	modularity	-	non-functional requirements
	well-defined components		
	minimal dependencies		
	increase workload		
	perform under failures		
[9]	Express the degree of goal satisfaction	-	-
	domain boundaries (scope)	-	-
	flexibility, generality, and robustness	-	
[7]	understandable and modifiable plans	-	-
	temporal constraints: relative and absolute	-	-
	flexibility, generality, and robustness	-	-
	Express the degree of goal satisfaction	-	-
[29]	efficiency/operationality	-	-
	maintenance and documentation	-	-
	clear and easy to understand by non-experts	-	-
[31]	encoding language	-	-
	semantic, syntactic, physical, pragmatic, and operational qualities	-	-
[27]	accuracy, adequacy, completeness, operationality, and consistency	-	-

References

1. Aiello, M., Fiorini, L., Georgievski, I.: Software engineering smart energy systems. In: Handbook of smart energy systems, pp. 1–29. Springer (2022). https://doi.org/10.1007/978-3-030-72322-4_21-1

2. Aiello, M., Pratt-Hartmann, I., Van Benthem, J.: What is spatial logic? Handbook of spatial logics pp. 1–11 (2007). https://doi.org/10.1007/978-1-4020-5587-4

3. Alnazer, E., Georgievski, I., Aiello, M.: On Bringing HTN Domains Closer to Reality - The Case of Satellite and Rover Domains

4. Alnazer, E., Georgievski, I., Aiello, M.: Risk Awareness in HTN Planning. arXiv preprint arXiv:2204.10669 (2022)

5. Alnazer, E., Georgievski, I., Prakash, N., Aiello, M.: A role for HTN planning in increasing trust in autonomous driving. In: ISC2, pp. 1–7. IEEE (2022). https://doi.org/10.1109/ISC255366.2022.9922427

6. Andréka, H., Madarász, J.X., Németi, I.: Logic of space-time and relativity theory. Handbook of spatial logics pp. 607–711 (2007). https://doi.org/10.1007/978-1-4020-5587-4_11

7. Chien, S., Hill, R., Jr., Wang, X., Estlin, T., Fayyad, K., Mortensen, H.: Why real-world planning is difficult: A tale of two applications. IOS Press, Washington, DC (1996)

8. Chrpa, L.: Modeling Planning Tasks: Representation Matters. KEPS pp. 107–123 (2020). https://doi.org/10.1007/978-3-030-38561-3_6

9. Evans, C., Brodie, L., Augusto, J.C.: Requirements engineering for intelligent environments. In: Intelligent Environments. pp. 154–161. IEEE (2014). https://doi.org/10.1109/IE.2014.30

10. Fiorini, L., Aiello, M.: Energy management for user's thermal and power needs: a survey. Energy Rep. **5**, 1048–1076 (2019). https://doi.org/10.1016/j.egyr.2019.08.003

11. Fiorini, L., Aiello, M.: Predictive multi-objective scheduling with dynamic prices and marginal CO_2-emission intensities. In: ACM e-Energy. pp. 196–207 (2020). https://doi.org/10.1145/3396851.3397732

12. Georgievski, I.: Coordinating services embedded everywhere via hierarchical planning (2015)

13. Georgievski, I.: Towards Engineering AI Planning Functionalities as Services. In: Service-Oriented Computing - ICSOC 2022 Workshops. pp. 225–236. LNCS, Springer (2022). https://doi.org/10.1007/978-3-031-26507-5_18

14. Georgievski, I.: Conceptualising software development lifecycle for engineering AI planning systems. In: CAIN (2023). https://doi.org/10.1109/CAIN58948.2023.00019

15. Georgievski, I., Aiello, M.: HTN planning: overview, comparison, and beyond. AIJ **222**, 124–156 (2015). https://doi.org/10.1016/j.artint.2015.02.002

16. Georgievski, I., Aiello, M.: Automated planning for ubiquitous computing. CSUR **49**(4), 1–46 (2016). https://doi.org/10.1145/3004294

17. Georgievski, I., Aiello, M.: Building automation based on temporal planning (2023)

18. Georgievski, I., Nguyen, T.A., Nizamic, F., Setz, B., Lazovik, A., Aiello, M.: Planning meets activity recognition: service coordination for intelligent buildings. PMC **38**, 110–139 (2017). https://doi.org/10.1016/j.pmcj.2017.02.008

19. Georgievski, I., Nizamic, F., Lazovik, A., Aiello, M.: Cloud ready applications composed via HTN planning. In: SOCA, pp. 81–89. IEEE (2017). https://doi.org/10.1109/SOCA.2017.19

20. Ghallab, M., Nau, D., Traverso, P.: Automated Planning: theory and practice. Elsevier (2004)

21. Glass, G., Hopkins, K.: Descriptive research in qualitative and quantitative research. J. Educ. Commun. Technol. **3**(1), 45–57 (1984). https://doi.org/10.1007/978-1-4615-1401-5_12

22. Gregory, P., Lindsay, A.: Domain model acquisition in domains with action costs. In: ICAPS, vol. 26, pp. 149–157 (2016). https://doi.org/10.1609/icaps.v26i1.13762
23. Hoffmann, J., Edelkamp, S., Thiébaux, S., Englert, R., Liporace, F., Trüg, S.: Engineering benchmarks for planning: the domains used in the deterministic part of IPC-4. JAIR **26**, 453–541 (2006). https://doi.org/10.1613/jair.1982
24. Kaldeli, E., Lazovik, A., Aiello, M.: Extended goals for composing services. In: ICAPS, vol. 19, pp. 362–365 (2009). https://doi.org/10.1609/icaps.v19i1.13385
25. Kaldeli, E., Warriach, E.U., Lazovik, A., Aiello, M.: Coordinating the web of services for a smart home. TWEB **7**(2), 1–40 (2013). https://doi.org/10.1145/2460383.2460389
26. Levermore, G.J.: Building energy management systems: applications to low-energy HVAC and natural ventilation control. Taylor & Francis (2000)
27. McCluskey, T.L., Vaquero, T.S., Vallati, M.: Engineering knowledge for automated planning: towards a notion of quality. In: K-CAP, pp. 1–8 (2017). https://doi.org/10.1145/3148011.3148012
28. McCluskey, T.L., Simpson, R.M.: Knowledge Formulation for AI Planning. In: Motta, E., Shadbolt, N.R., Stutt, A., Gibbins, N. (eds.) EKAW 2004. LNCS (LNAI), vol. 3257, pp. 449–465. Springer, Heidelberg (2004). https://doi.org/10.1007/978-3-540-30202-5_30
29. Shah, M., et al.: Knowledge engineering tools in planning: state-of-the-art and future challenges. KEPS **53**, 53 (2013)
30. Silva, J.R., Silva, J.M., Vaquero, T.S.: Formal Knowledge Engineering for Planning: Pre and Post-Design Analysis. In: Vallati, M., Kitchin, D. (eds.) Knowledge Engineering Tools and Techniques for AI Planning, pp. 47–65. Springer, Cham (2020). https://doi.org/10.1007/978-3-030-38561-3_3
31. Vallati, M., McCluskey, L.: A quality framework for automated planning knowledge models. In: Agents and Artificial Intelligence, pp. 635–644. SciTePress (2021). https://doi.org/10.5220/0010216806350644
32. Vallati, M., McCluskey, T.L.: In Defence of Design Patterns for AI Planning Knowledge Models. In: Baldoni, M., Bandini, S. (eds.) AIxIA 2020. LNCS (LNAI), vol. 12414, pp. 191–203. Springer, Cham (2021). https://doi.org/10.1007/978-3-030-77091-4_12
33. Vaquero, T.S., Silva, J.R., Tonidandel, F., Beck, J.C.: itSIMPLE: towards an integrated design system for real planning applications. Knowl. Eng. Rev. **28**(2), 215–230 (2013). https://doi.org/10.1017/S0269888912000434
34. Vaquero, T.S., Silva, J.R., Beck, J.C.: Improving planning performance through post-design analysis. In: KEPS, pp. 45–52 (2010)
35. Wazlawick, R.S.: Reflections about research in computer science regarding the classification of sciences and the scientific method. FSMA **6**, 3–10 (2010)
36. Weser, M., Off, D., Zhang, J.: HTN robot planning in partially observable dynamic environments. In: ICRA, pp. 1505–1510. IEEE (2010). https://doi.org/10.1109/ROBOT.2010.5509770

Empowering Machine Learning Development with Service-Oriented Computing Principles

Mostafa Hadadian Nejad Yousefi[1], Viktoriya Degeler[2],
and Alexander Lazovik[1(✉)]

[1] Faculty of Science and Engineering, Bernoulli Institute, University of Groningen,
Groningen, The Netherlands
{m.hadadian,a.lazovik}@rug.nl
[2] Faculty of Science, Informatics Institute, University of Amsterdam, Amsterdam,
The Netherlands
v.o.degeler@uva.nl

Abstract. Despite software industries' successful utilization of Service-Oriented Computing (SOC) to streamline software development, machine learning (ML) development has yet to fully integrate these practices. This disparity can be attributed to multiple factors, such as the unique challenges inherent to ML development and the absence of a unified framework for incorporating services into this process. In this paper, we shed light on the disparities between services-oriented computing and machine learning development. We propose "Everything as a Module" (XaaM), a framework designed to encapsulate every ML artifacts including models, code, data, and configurations as individual modules, to bridge this gap. We propose a set of additional steps that need to be taken to empower machine learning development using services-oriented computing via an architecture that facilitates efficient management and orchestration of complex ML systems. By leveraging the best practices of services-oriented computing, we believe that machine learning development can achieve a higher level of maturity, improve the efficiency of the development process, and ultimately, facilitate the more effective creation of machine learning applications.

Keywords: Machine Learning Lifecycle · MLOps · Service-Oriented Computing · Adaptive Data Processing · ML Pipelines

1 Introduction

Machine learning (ML) has emerged as a powerful tool for solving complex problems across various domains, leading to a growing demand for production-grade ML applications. With the increasing importance of ML in various industries, the need for efficient and scalable ML development has become more pronounced.

M. Aiello et al. (Eds.): SummerSOC 2023, CCIS 1847, pp. 24–44, 2023.
https://doi.org/10.1007/978-3-031-45728-9_2

However, despite the rapid advancements in ML techniques and tools, the development of production-grade ML systems still faces several challenges that hinder its alignment with best practices in software development [25].

In recent years, the software industry has successfully embraced service-oriented computing (SOC) and DevOps ("Development Operations" to automate software development process), which has significantly improved software development processes, enabling better modularity, flexibility, and maintainability [31]. However, ML development has not yet fully adopted these best practices, resulting in a gap between service-oriented computing and ML development [1].

DevOps is a cross-departmental and collaborative endeavor within an organization, aiming to simplify the continuous delivery of new software releases while upholding their integrity and trustworthiness [26]. In service-oriented computing, DevOps is a cultural shift and set of practices for enhancing collaboration between development and operations teams. This approach accelerates the development life cycle for efficient, continuous software service delivery. DevOps incorporates Agile principles, e.g., continuous integration, deployment, and automated testing, which are critical in service-oriented computing for integration and constant service availability. Moreover, DevOps encourages improved communication and collaboration across service production and maintenance teams.

MLOps (Machine Learning Operations) can be considered an extension of DevOps. It applies the principles and practices of DevOps to the specific challenges and requirements of machine learning development. This includes the development, deployment, and lifecycle management of ML models, while addressing the complexities inherent in data-driven machine learning.

Challenges in MLOps stem from the unique nature of machine learning models. For instance, they may degrade over time as data drifts occur, requiring constant monitoring and frequent retraining. Another challenge is managing the lifecycle of a machine learning model, which includes stages like data collection, model training, validation, deployment, and continuous monitoring. Moreover, another common challenge is the reproducibility of ML models due to variations in data, code, configuration, or environment, which can lead to inconsistencies in model performance. MLOps aims to address these challenges by providing a robust framework for managing the ML lifecycle, similar to how DevOps manages the software development lifecycle. It incorporates practices like versioning of datasets and ML models, automated testing, and continuous integration/continuous delivery (CI/CD) for machine learning models to ensure their reliability and performance over time.

In this paper, we investigate the best practices in service-oriented computing and DevOps and identify the gaps between these practices and machine learning development and MLOps. Inspired by Anything as a Service (XaaS), we propose our "Everything as a Module" (XaaM) vision, an enabler of MLOps practices and a comprehensive solution for bridging these gaps. In this vision, we encapsulate every machine learning artifact such as model, code, data, and configurations as a module. XaaM is specifically introduced to differentiate between conventional web services and machine learning services, while also catering to the machine learning community's preference for the term "Module". However, XaaM is different from XaaS which is a business and delivery model that provides various types of services over the Internet. These services could range from Infrastructure (IaaS), Platform (PaaS), to Software (SaaS), and beyond.

The contributions of this research, reflecting our vision, are as follows. First, we present the concept of two levels of modularity, elaborating on the definition of modules, while addressing polymorphism. We then describe our approach to composing complex modules from atomic ones. We also highlight the importance of module versioning for experiment tracking in machine learning applications, with the aim of achieving maximum observability. Here, our intention is to create a system where every artifact is trackable throughout the development process, a goal we strive to achieve through the introduction of module lineage.

Subsequently, we venture into the challenge of monitoring machine learning applications, providing our perspective on managing the lifecycle of modules. This is realized by proposing Adaptive Module Selection and What-if Scenarios. The former aspires to select the most effective module at any given time, while the latter is akin to automatic testing to facilitate improved module evaluation.

This work encapsulates our vision to enhance machine learning development by leveraging the best practices from service-oriented computing, thereby leading to the creation of more robust, efficient, and scalable ML systems. While we anticipate benefits such as improved development efficiency, increased scalability and adaptability of ML applications, and more effective creation of production-grade ML systems, these outcomes depend on a successful implementation of our proposals. One of the motivational goals of our vision is fostering interdepartmental communication and collaboration by advocating a modular design. Note that our work presents a blueprint towards a desired state, not a fully functioning system. We aim to advance machine learning development practices and encourage more widespread use of service-oriented computing in this field.

The rest of this paper is structured as follows: Sect. 2 offers background for a better understanding of service-oriented computing and machine learning development. Section 3 presents a review of related work. Section 4 identifies the gaps that exist in various aspects and proposes solutions to bridge them. Finally, Sect. 5 presents our conclusions.

2   Background

2.1   Service-Oriented Computing

Service-Oriented Computing (SOC) is a distributed computing paradigm that utilizes services as building blocks for applications [31]. These services are often realized as web services or microservices which can be described, published, located, and invoked over a network. This paradigm promotes interoperability, integration, and simplifies large-scale system development, reducing complexity via service reuse and advancing business agility and innovation.

In technical terms, these services are commonly encapsulated within containers, such as Docker, to ensure their isolation and to simplify their deployment and scaling. Management and orchestration of these containers can be achieved using technologies like Kubernetes, which enables automated deployment, scaling, and management, effectively distributing and coordinating containers across a cluster of machines [8]. Communication among these services, vital for orchestrating complex business processes, leverages protocols like HTTP/REST or gRPC for synchronous, and message brokers for asynchronous communication.

2.2 Machine Learning Development

Drawing from literature [37, 41], we synthesize the common elements into a generalized workflow of lifecycle of Artificial Intelligence/Machine Learning (AI/ML) applications depicted in Fig. 1.

Fig. 1. Coarse-grained AI/ML application life-cycle illustrating the stages and their corresponding actors.

The AI/ML lifecycle encompasses five interrelated stages. First, during the *business requirement* stage, stakeholders collaborate with the AI/ML team to define the problem, objectives, and project scope. Second, the *data preparation* stage entails acquiring, cleaning, preprocessing, and transforming data for model training and evaluation. Third, the *AI/ML development* stage focuses on designing, implementing, and validating machine learning models. Fourth, the *application deployment* stage integrates models into an application, ensuring its stability, performance, and security in an operational environment. Finally, the *monitoring stage* involves tracking the application's performance, identifying issues, and gathering insights for continuous improvement.

AI/ML development diverges from traditional software development, primarily due to its data-driven nature. It involves iteratively constructing probabilistic models that learn patterns from data, a process that requires extensive experimentation and monitoring. Teams often explore various model architectures and algorithms before settling on a solution. Moreover, decisions are data-driven, emphasizing the quality of the data used for model training. Evaluating a learning model is a complex task, as its performance is tightly coupled with the data. Thus, teams must conduct extensive training and testing on both small and large datasets that closely resemble production data, necessitating a scalable underlying platform. Throughout this process, monitoring and experiment tracking become critical to compare different models, observe their performance over time, and ensure reproducibility. The latter means that running the same model with the same data should ideally yield the same results, despite the inherent probabilistic nature of ML models. This iterative, monitored, and reproducible process ensures that the AI/ML solution generalizes well to new, unseen data and effectively addresses the defined business requirements.

3 Related Work

This section focuses on MLOps and the study of solutions founded on the principles of service-oriented computing for machine learning. For convenience and cohesion, we discuss other relevant subjects in their sections. Our dual goal is to highlight the differences between ML development and SOC, and to centralize related content for easy access and reference.

MLOps is an emerging paradigm, merging machine learning and traditional software development using DevOps principles. It focuses on automating machine learning development, deployment, and monitoring to boost efficiency and shorten time to market [37]. Testi et al. [41] respond to the fragmented state of MLOps literature by proposing a cohesive taxonomy and standardized methodology for MLOps projects. Several studies address MLOps challenges and solution to facilitate this integration.

Symeonidis et al. [40] delve into the complexities of Machine Learning Operations (MLOps), highlighting challenges like efficient pipeline creation, continual model re-training, comprehensive monitoring, and data manipulation. They discuss tools for data preprocessing, modeling, and operationalization, highlighting AutoML's potential to automate and simplify the machine learning process. Granlund et al. [18] discuss AI/ML operations' integration challenges, focusing on complexities of data consolidation, shared ML model development, and cross-organizational system performance monitoring. They also discuss the scaling challenge related to managing data from multiple entities, developing personalized models, and providing tailored monitoring options in a large, multi-organizational setting. Zhou et al. [44] use existing CI/CD tools and Kubeflow to illuminate potential performance bottlenecks like GPU utilization. Their analysis of time and resource consumption in ML pipelines offers a practical guide for efficient ML pipeline platform construction.

Another interesting area is applying microservices architecture in ML development [10]. Microservices enable the modularization of ML components, allowing for more flexible development and deployment of ML applications. This method also encourages reusability of components, significantly saving development time and effort. Several studies cover machine-learning use for service-oriented computing, but few investigated the integration of machine learning models into service-oriented architectures. Fantinato et al. [15] review the mutual enhancement of service-oriented architecture (SOA) and deep learning. They detail how deep learning aids SOA solutions using web service data and how SOA enables flexible, reusable infrastructures for deep learning. Their study highlights the potential of this synergy for various environments and users, shedding light on these technologies' evolution. Briese et al. [7] propose a service-oriented architecture for rapid deployment of deep learning in reverse logistics, addressing the problem of uninterpretable markers. Their method allows using ever-expanding, initially small datasets, reducing digitization and labeling costs and time.

Mboweni et al. [28] extensively studied MLOps literature to identify the state-of-the-art and gaps in understanding. Despite abundant literature, their review uncovers a lack of standardization and a shared vision on implementing MLOps across industries, showing a need for further research in this area. While these works offer insights into applying service-oriented computing in machine learning development, they often concentrate on specifics like MLOps or microservices, rather than a holistic vision for enhancing machine learning development using service-oriented computing principles. In this paper, we aim to broaden the perspective on this topic, discussing a variety of techniques to bridge the gap between machine learning development and service-oriented computing.

4   Methods

In this section, we examine various aspects of software development and identify existing gaps, using service-oriented computing as a reference point. We begin by introducing our perspective of modules and explaining module composition since these components form the fundamental pillars of our vision. Prior to delving into other constituent components, we present an overarching overview of our system. Subsequently, we explain each component in a more intricate manner.

4.1   Modularity by Design

Modularity by design refers to an approach that emphasizes the creation of smaller, independent, and interchangeable services. These services can be assembled, rearranged, or replaced without affecting the overall system's functionality. The primary advantages of modular design include increased flexibility, reusability, maintainability, and scalability.

In our research, we distinguish between two levels of modularity within the context of machine learning applications: 1) Algorithmic Modularity and 2) Architectural Modularity. This classification highlights different aspects of machine learning applications, ranging from programming and code-level details to larger-scale system architecture and deployment considerations.

Algorithmic Modularity pertains to the utilization of programming languages or frameworks for the development of machine learning applications. Data scientists often employ frameworks such as Scikit-learn[1] or PyTorch[2] to facilitate various stages of their ML applications, including data preprocessing, scaling, modeling, and evaluation. Leveraging these frameworks enables the effective modularization of ML applications and accelerates the development process.

Architectural Modularity, on the other hand, involves packaging each stage into distinct services and deploying these services into appropriate environments, such as production. This modularity offers greater flexibility, improved

---

[1] https://scikit-learn.org/.
[2] https://pytorch.org/.

maintainability, and enhanced scalability, ensuring that the ML application remains adaptable to changing requirements and emerging technologies.

Due to the wealth of available frameworks in machine learning development, algorithmic modularity is well-established. AI/ML teams generally concentrate on the primary purpose of their applications and wish to avoid unnecessary complexities, such as packaging (e.g., containerization) or deployment [29]. They often create monolithic applications that may be deployed using services but remain monolithic by design, failing to exploit modularity's full potential.

As architectural modularity is less widespread, our primary goal is to promote its adoption and increase its prevalence in the field. Architectural modularity provides numerous benefits, including enhanced maintainability, scalability, and adaptability to changing requirements. By advocating for its adoption, we aim to facilitate the development of more robust and flexible ML applications.

In addition to the applicability, our proposed solution must be both user-friendly and easy to understand to ensure its acceptance within the community. Our approach aims to facilitate the seamless integration of services, promote efficient collaboration between different teams, and simplify the development process. To achieve this, we define modules as a higher abstraction of services with two main components rooted in the concept of polymorphism: Module Definition and Module Implementation. These components ensure applicability and enhance understandability by providing a clear separation between high-level and low-level information of a module.

Module Definition involves creating a general and unified interface for modules, similar to APIs for services. These interfaces facilitate communication among team members and between different teams, ensuring everyone has a clear understanding of each module, e.g. what are its purpose, inputs, and outputs. The clarity of module definition enables a better division of responsibilities. For instance, a clear module definition allows AI/ML teams to focus on the internal logic of modules, while DevOps teams handle packaging and deployment.

Module Implementation refers to the process of putting a module definition into practice, much like how concrete classes in object-oriented programming languages implement abstract classes. This method permits multiple implementations of a single module definition, fostering reusability and polymorphism within the system. Importantly, a module implementation can be composed of multiple smaller modules.

Throughout the remainder of this paper, we will use the term "module" to refer to services in the context of our research. Specifically, we will focus on machine learning services that are designed, implemented, and maintained using MLOps best practices, as well as the solutions we propose. We selected the term "module" due to its common usage in the machine learning field, where it denotes a self-contained and coherent unit of work that shares similarities with the concept of a service.

In essence, any combination of a module definition and module implementation forms a module, as illustrated in Fig. 3a. It is important to note that the definitions and implementations of the modules are loosely coupled. If a module implementation fulfills a module definition, they can be combined to create a module. Consequently, a single module definition may be satisfied by multiple implementations, and a module implementation may satisfy more than one definition. This flexibility is a significant advantage of our approach.

Modules that share the same module definition are considered equivalent, as they achieve the same objective. However, it is essential to acknowledge that equivalent modules may display different performances when handling the same tasks due to the variability in their implementations.

To illustrate, let us consider an example of a module definition and two module implementations. Imagine a module definition called "Scaler" where the input is a matrix of numeric data with shape (`n-samples`, `n-features`), and the output is a standardized version of this matrix with the same shape. The first implementation, "StandardScaler", standardizes the input features to have zero mean and unit variance. The second implementation, "MinMaxScaler" Rescales the input features to a specified range (usually [0, 1]). Although both implementations are scaling the input features, their output has a different distribution.

We propose a new concept called Everything as a Module (XaaM), which presents a general unified interface that facilitates the encapsulation of diverse components in an ML system, including executable codes, ML pipelines, and datasets. Figure 2 offers a demonstrative example of XaaM for the training and inference stages of an ML application, where each artifact is considered a module.

Using various implementations, XaaM enhances the modularity and flexibility of AI/ML applications, ultimately advancing the state-of-the-art and advancing innovation in the field.

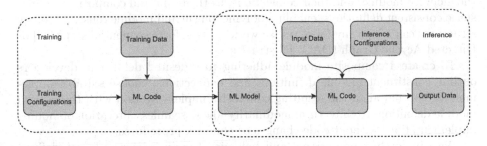

Fig. 2. An example XaaM demonstration for training and inference

4.2   Module Composition

Module composition is the process of combining simpler modules to form a more complex one, enabling developers to break down intricate systems into manageable components. Our goal is to create modular and adaptable modules that can be easily adjusted and extended to meet evolving requirements. Similar to Web Service Composition [3], we define two module types:

- **Atomic Module**: A self-contained module independent of other modules, such as a Docker container.
- **Composite Module**: A module composed of multiple atomic or composite modules, like a data processing pipeline consisting of Scaler and Model modules, as shown in Fig. 3c.

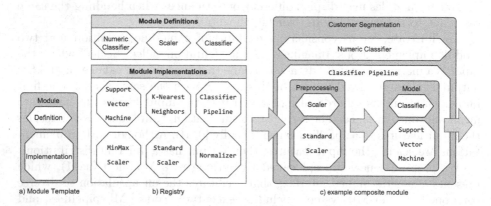

Fig. 3. Module Composition Example: a) Module template, b) Sample registry, c) A composite module from registry elements, adhering to the given template.

Our framework houses module definitions and implementations in a registry (Fig. 3b). A composite module is represented by a graph topology, which details the included modules and their connections. Both atomic and composite modules share consistent definitions, enabling polymorphism and module reuse. Topology structures can adopt any form, unlike works that enforce sequential steps [43] or Directed Acyclic Graph (DAG) [5] structure.

To create a composite module adhering to a desired definition, developers outline constituent module definitions and connections, choose suitable implementations, and align the resulting composite implementation with the desired module definition. Architectural modularity allows seamless alteration of module implementations without code changes or complex procedures.

We can conduct operational and behavioral verifications with well-defined module structures. Operational verification confirms the pipeline's correctness, while behavioral verification assesses whether the composite module produces the expected output. The former relies on module implementations, and the latter depends on module definitions.

We propose two automation stages for module composition: 1) Topology Creation and 2) Implementation Selection. The first stage generates a topology using modules from the registry or creating missing module definitions. The second stage selects appropriate implementations for each definition, ensuring that the chosen implementations can interact effectively and process data efficiently.

Module composition in machine learning development differs from service composition due to its probabilistic nature. Performance cannot be guaranteed through testing on available data alone, but we can use historical data and feedback to make informed decisions during module composition.

There are several techniques available for the automation of machine learning application creation, such as AutoAI [9] and AutoML [19]. While these approaches hold significant promise, they are not without their challenges, as identified by Elshawi et al. [14]. In our work, we aim to address several of these challenges, including Composability, Scalability, and Continuous delivery pipeline.

One of the primary challenges with existing AutoAI and AutoML approaches is their lack of generality and flexibility, particularly with respect to composability. These approaches often lack the ability to incorporate custom components or allow users to tweak the generated machine learning pipeline. Our approach aims to address this limitation by providing a fully automated solution that is still general enough to allow users to be involved in various formats. For instance, users can define certain parts of a composite module and let the system fill in the rest, allowing for greater flexibility and customizability.

In addition to addressing the issue of composability, we also seek to tackle challenges related to scalability, which can be especially problematic for large real datasets. To overcome this challenge, we plan to utilize techniques such as meta-learning to learn from previous runs and gradually improve the composite module's performance. This aligns with our goal of establishing a continuous delivery pipeline for machine learning applications, enabling us to deliver more effective solutions to end-users while improving overall efficiency and scalability.

In summary, our approach to module composition provides greater composability, flexibility, and scalability, allowing for more customized and adaptable machine learning pipelines. By leveraging historical data and feedback, we can make more informed decisions during module composition, which contributes to the continuous improvement of the composite module's performance. Ultimately, our approach allows for the development of more effective machine learning applications while reducing development time and costs.

4.3 Proposed Architecture

We propose a simplified layered architecture that serves as an overview of the implementation of our vision illustrated in Fig. 4. The ultimate goal is to enable users to define module definitions and the system takes care of the rest including automatically associating it with proper implementations and deploying the modules. In this section, we will explore the different components of the proposed architecture and their interactions.

The version control component is the entry point to the system where users can add module definitions and module implementations to the registry. A proper versioning mechanism enables observability, extensive experiment tracking, and module lineage. In particular, it is essential for other components such as monitoring and adaptive module selection to fully operate. Therefore, to avoid overcomplicating other components' mechanisms, we propose a unified versioning mechanism for every module.

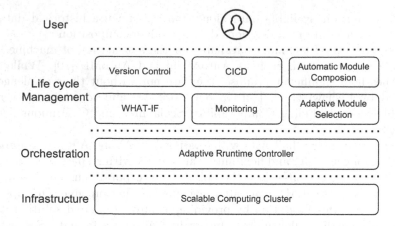

Fig. 4. A layered architecture implements the XaaM vision, with items in each layer interacting only with adjacent layer items.

From this point the Continuous Integration and Continuous Deployment (CI/CD) pipeline is responsible for managing the automatic workflow of delivering module definitions from the registry to an environment among other responsibilities. This pipeline invokes the automatic module composition and selection components in order to complete modules by selecting or generating module implementations for the module definitions while testing different scenarios via the What-If component. Finally, it invokes the adaptive runtime controller for deploying the module on the underlying infrastructure.

The automatic module composition process creates placeholders for module implementations and leverages adaptive module selection to fill them at design time. This process may involve multiple iterations if a valid selection is not found. If no solution is found, the automatic module composition returns an incomplete module to the user, identifying the missing implementations.

Once a module is ready, meaning that at least one module implementation satisfies the module definition, it is submitted to the adaptive runtime controller for deployment in the cluster. Users can also define monitoring modules and bind them to other modules, such as inference modules. One of the key features of our platform and the XaaM vision is the ability to have monitoring modules that monitor other monitoring modules within the cluster.

The what-if component is responsible for generating scenarios for various purposes, such as testing and interpretability. It submits these scenarios to the adaptive runtime controller, which runs them in separate environments to avoid interference with production systems.

Monitoring modules collect data on the performance of other modules and store it in a standardized format for multiple purposes, such as visualization in a graphical interface. The adaptive module selection component actively checks the monitoring data and updates the module implementations accordingly to satisfy the requirement that may come from the user or a downstream module. This comprehensive monitoring system ensures that the platform remains efficient, adaptive, and responsive to changing requirements and conditions.

The adaptive runtime controller component is responsible for continuously syncing the actual state of the scalable computing cluster with the desired state. We develop our control mechanism on top of Kubernetes which is an open-source container orchestration system that can operate on a diverse range of infrastructures such as Amazon AWS[3] and Google Cloud Platform[4]. This implementation makes our system portable and avoids vendor lock-in. Finally, the scalable computing cluster is where the modules run.

4.4   Version Control

Version control is essential in both software engineering and machine learning, managing artifacts like source code, configuration files, and documentation in the former [45], and tracking changes in data, models, hyperparameters, and code in the latter [6]. Effective version control systems facilitate collaboration, reproducibility, and debugging.

Git has become the industry standard in version control for software engineering, with popular implementations like GitHub, GitLab, and BitBucket. It can manage common artifacts in machine learning, such as hyperparameters stored as plain text. However, managing large datasets and model weights presents unique challenges such as lack of standardization [21] and intricacies involved in tracking and recording model changes, leading to problems like reproducibility and model comparison [20].

To address these challenges, specialized version control systems such as DVC[5], Pachyderm[6], and MLflow[7] have been developed. They offer features like model versioning, data versioning, and model lineage tracking, simplifying the management of model and data updates. Cloud-based solutions like Amazon S3, Azure Blob Storage, and Google Cloud Storage can provide scalable storage and versioning solutions for large models and datasets.

In our XaaM vision, we treat data and other components as modules, ensuring consistency across various projects and teams. We store module definitions and implementations in an informative text format, i.e., YAML (YAML Ain't Markup Language), enabling Git-based version control on a metadata level. Module definitions are stored fully in YAML format since they are designed to be describable in text format. On the other hand, module implementations are more complex as they can have various forms. Therefore, we designed a unified YAML description that captures features of the implementation. This YAML file is then linked to the actual implementation.

---

[3] https://aws.amazon.com/.
[4] https://cloud.google.com/.
[5] https://dvc.org/.
[6] https://www.pachyderm.com/.
[7] https://mlflow.org/.

Within our XaaM vision, we adopt a modular approach where every ML asset encompassing data, code, models, and executables are treated as distinct modules, thereby ensuring a cohesive framework across diverse projects and teams. We establish a registry of module definitions and implementations in an informative text format, specifically YAML, which facilitates version control through Git at a metadata level. The module definitions are exclusively stored in YAML to align with their text-based descriptive nature. Conversely, module implementations necessitate a more comprehensive treatment due to their multifaceted nature. To address this, we have devised a comprehensive YAML schema that encapsulates the nuances of the implementation. This specialized YAML file is linked to the tangible implementation, facilitating a unified and coherent framework. This method streamlines project administration, guarantees uniformity, and eases the integration of varied modules and tools, thereby fostering the creation of intricate, scalable machine learning solutions.

Our cohesive XaaM versioning approach significantly enhances both transparency and reproducibility within the context of module development. This is achieved through the comprehensive preservation of module lineage, encompassing every facet from data and code to configuration settings, that contributed to creating each module. Put simply, this framework empowers users to carefully trace the trajectory and evolution of individual modules within the project. For example, users possess the capability to discern the origins of output data, encompassing details such as the model employed, configuration parameters utilized, and input data employed during its generation.

Ultimately, our approach allows for the targeted application of techniques aligned with each unique implementation, all within the framework of our YAML-based versioning system. By leveraging both traditional version control systems like Git and specialized tools tailored for machine learning, we bridge the gap between machine learning development and software development, ultimately leading to more effective and streamlined machine learning projects with enhanced transparency and reproducibility through module lineage tracking.

4.5   Continuous Monitoring

Continuous monitoring is vital for managing application health and performance in software development projects, particularly in service-based applications with complex interdependencies [13]. In machine learning projects, continuous monitoring is even more critical since it ensures model performance remains consistent, detects data drift, anomalies, and performance issues [41], and determines when model retraining is necessary [22].

Challenges in continuous monitoring include integrating monitoring metrics and KPI evaluations from different teams [41], scalability and real-time monitoring [39], addressing the statistical nature of drift detection and outlier identification [24], standardization data collection and storage methods [30], and monitoring upstream processes that feed data to ML systems [39]. Our XaaM vision addresses these challenges by building on state-of-the-art monitoring techniques that adapt to changing requirements and workloads without adversely affecting performance.

We propose **Monitoring as a Module** to integrate various monitoring techniques and enable seamless collaboration between teams. Monitoring modules are treated almost the same way as other modules. The only difference is the way of handling modules by the adaptive runtime controller which employs specific mechanisms to collect data from other modules seamlessly and redirect the output data to a standard storage. Subsequently, the monitoring team can develop the monitoring module definition and implementation in the same way as other modules. They can also benefit from the automation offered by our system to create composite monitoring modules automatically that deliver the desired functionality. It is also worth mentioning that since the monitoring modules are the same as other modules, they can also be monitored using other monitoring modules.

We introduce the concept of Monitoring as a Module, which serves as an integration point for diverse monitoring methodologies, fostering harmonious collaboration among teams. Monitoring modules are treated almost the same way as other modules. A nuanced distinction lies in the manner by which these modules interface with the adaptive runtime controller. This controller employs distinct mechanisms to seamlessly fetch information from concurrent modules, channeling output data to a standardized repository.

Consequently, the monitoring team finds themselves capacitated to devise module definitions and implementations for monitoring on par with general module practices. Leveraging the automation inherent to our framework, they are further empowered to fabricate composite monitoring modules. Moreover, it is worth mentioning that the equivalence of monitoring modules with other modules extends to the realm of monitoring, wherein monitoring modules themselves are amenable to oversight through analogous monitoring modules. This confers the capability for adaptive module selection to not merely ensure the fulfillment of requirements by the monitored modules, but also to maintain the monitoring modules' correctness. Ultimately, this synergy culminates in an enhanced performance exhibited by the monitored modules.

4.6   Adaptive Module Selection

Module selection involves searching and identifying module implementations that align with a specific module definition and its requirements, resembling service composition in web services. In our vision, selection emphasizes choosing existing implementations, while composition focuses on generating new modules. This process can occur at three stages in the module composition life cycle: design time, deployment time, and runtime.

During design time, developers create and define a module tailored to fulfill specific requirements. Deployment time involves installing and configuring the composition in the runtime environment for execution. Runtime is when the module is executed, and its performance and functionality are evaluated. Module selection at runtime depends on algorithms that associate module definitions with implementations based on performance metrics and requirements, ensuring the selection of the most suitable implementation.

Service selection algorithms prioritize QoS attributes such as response time, success rate, and cost [11]. In machine learning development, we must ensure QoS metrics while satisfying performance requirements, like accuracy and Mean Squared Error (MSE) [17]. Addressing the interdependence of metrics is crucial, considering modules correlations and user requirements correlations [27, 33].

Our vision's module selection consists of three primary stages, each presenting unique challenges:

- **candidating:** find suitable module implementations for a module definition.
- **ranking**: order top-performing module implementations for a scenario.
- **choosing**: determine if updating the production module is worthwhile.

Challenges during the *candidating* phase include ensuring implementation satisfaction of the module definition and designing a scalable find-matching algorithm. The level of granularity poses another challenge, as a module implementation may be a composite module. In our vision, find-matching algorithms' input is the YAML-based descriptions of module definition and implementation. Analogous to web-service selection [16], we incorporate the structural-semantic approach enhances the candidate identification phase, using domain ontology concepts, similarity measures, and structural properties analysis to select suitable module implementations.

Defining the scenario presents a significant challenge during the *ranking* stage, given its reliance on variable factors such as incoming data streams, sensing and operational environments, and requirements. The subsequent difficulty lies in forecasting future scenarios and the corresponding performance of each individual module within these hypothetical situations. In our vision, we propose a pipeline incorporating a scenario prediction algorithm and a metamodel. This metamodel is designed to estimate module performance utilizing the historical data collected via monitoring modules.

Finally, the *choosing* phase entails the critical decision of whether to update the existing module in the production environment, taking into account the costs of redeployment and possible non-optimal performance measures. The effectiveness of this phase is inextricably linked to the successful execution of the ranking stage and the accuracy of future scenario prediction. Furthermore, it must take into account the distinct overheads and deployment costs that may be associated with different modules.

Designing a reliable and fast adaptive module selection involves numerous interconnected choices across all phases. Understanding these choices' influence on each other and the overall system performance is essential. A holistic approach is necessary to create a system that can adapt effectively to changing scenarios and maintain optimal performance across various scenarios.

4.7 Life Cycle Management

Software life cycle management covers stages from inception to maintenance of a software product. This process ensures software meets user and stakeholder requirements, adheres to quality standards, and fits cost constraints [23]. Differences in life cycle management between machine learning (ML) and traditional software development stem from ML's data reliance and iterative model training, contrasted with traditional software development's deterministic approach.

In ML development, data is crucial throughout the entire life cycle, with data collection, preprocessing, and feature engineering significantly affecting model performance [39]. Model training in ML development involves iterative experimentation with algorithms, hyperparameters, and data representations [34]. Validation and testing in ML development involve assessing model generalization to unseen data, which can be challenging due to overfitting and biases [36]. Deploying an ML model requires serving it in a production environment, monitoring its performance, and updating or fine-tuning it as necessary [4].

Traditional software development has adopted CI/CD practices, but ML development still faces challenges in integrating these practices due to the iterative nature of model training and dependency on data [32]. Emerging tools such as MLflow [43], TFX [4], and Kubeflow [5] address the unique requirements of ML CI/CD but still leave room for improvement in aligning these practices with traditional software development. Ensuring explainable predictions is crucial for gaining user trust and ensuring ethical use in ML development [2].

Our vision incorporates "What-if" scenarios [35] into ML development to facilitate validation, testing, and interpretability. Sensitivity analysis can help identify potential weaknesses or areas of improvement and inform the selection of features and parameters [38]. Counterfactual explanations provide insights into how a model might behave if specific features or inputs were different, supporting better decision-making and model understanding [42]. Automatic scenario generation techniques allow developers to consider multiple plausible future scenarios and their potential impacts on ML models or software systems to inform model development and decision-making.

The What-If scenario component plays a crucial role in our vision, encompassing a range of possibilities that significantly enhance our machine learning module's adaptability and robustness.

Firstly, It engages with the aspect of "new data vs current modules". In essence, it consistently explores the hypothetical question, "What if an alternative equivalent module was operational instead of the currently running one?" This means that it generates various scenarios where any active module is replaced by an equivalent alternative, contributing to the system's adaptability.

Secondly, it contemplates "new modules vs historical data". Whenever a new module is introduced, the component seeks to answer, "What if these modules were already integrated into our system?" This implies that it measures the performance of the newcomer against collected historical data. This is accomplished either by running the new module or estimating its performance. This provision of the What-If scenario component aids in adaptive module selection, generating more data to enhance performance.

Lastly, it examines the interaction of "current modules vs unseen data". Unlike traditional software development, machine learning development does not allow for extensive testing. To counter this limitation, the What-If scenario component learns from the shortcomings of other equivalent modules, generating corner-case scenarios to test modules against any unforeseen circumstances. This not only ensures model robustness but also facilitates proactive identification of potential issues, significantly improving the system's resilience.

This component greatly aid in the process of adaptive module selection, enabling the system to collect more data and consequently perform more effectively. Ultimately, incorporating what-if scenarios in ML and traditional software development can help bridge the gap between these domains by enhancing model understanding and improving decision-making.

4.8   Adaptive Runtime Controller

A runtime controller is a software component responsible for managing and orchestrating the execution of applications or services at runtime. It ensures that the desired state of the system is maintained and adapts to any changes or requirements that may arise during the execution. Kubernetes, a widely adopted platform for orchestrating containerized services, has emerged as a best practice in this context [8]. It offers numerous built-in features and solutions that simplify application deployment, scaling, and management.

Machine learning development and our adaptive module selection require frequent changes in the modules, depending on various factors such as the application's needs, user preferences, or environmental conditions. Kubernetes provides a mechanism called the operator pattern, which can be used to implement this adaptive behavior [12]. An operator is a custom controller that extends the functionality of the Kubernetes API by implementing custom control logic and defining custom resource definitions (CRDs), which are stored in YAML format.

We designed CRDs to possess a one-to-one correspondence with module definitions and implementation, thereby making them straightforward and user-friendly. This allows users to specify their requirements with minimal technical acumen. In other words, the user-defined module definitions and implementations serve as the direct input to the controller, which represents the desired state. The controller then translates this high-level desired state into technical specifications. Kubernetes CRDs are translated into OpenAPI APIs, enabling seamless integration with the Kubernetes API server.

The controller continually monitors the actual state of the system in the cluster and attempts to match it with the desired state defined by the user. We implemented modules, consisting of both module definition and module implementation, as Kubernetes CRDs. To support deploying modules as a service and adaptive module selection mechanism, we developed several custom controllers that extend the Kubernetes API. These custom controllers manage various aspects of the system, such as container deployment, storage, and communication.

However, since it is impossible to cover every possible deployment need and to ensure the generality of our platform, we designed our CRD in a way that allows more advanced users to develop their own custom controllers. These custom controllers can be used in a pluggable fashion, enabling users to tailor the adaptive runtime controller to their specific needs and requirements. This flexibility allows for a wide range of use cases and applications, making the adaptive runtime controller a powerful tool for managing complex, dynamic systems.

In summary, the adaptive runtime controller leverages the power of Kubernetes and the operator pattern to provide a flexible and extensible platform for managing and orchestrating modules in various applications. By designing user-friendly CRDs and supporting custom controllers, the adaptive runtime controller enables users to implement complex adaptive behavior with ease, ultimately leading to more robust and responsive systems.

5   Conclusion

In this paper, we presented the "Everything as a Module" (XaaM) vision, a comprehensive approach that aims to empower machine learning development by addressing the unique challenges in machine learning and deviations from the best practices of service-oriented software development. We investigated several aspects, identified the gaps, and proposed solutions for bridging these gaps.

We also introduced an architecture to demonstrate how the various components of the XaaM vision can be seamlessly integrated, enabling users to efficiently manage and orchestrate complex systems. We believe that the XaaM vision has the potential to revolutionize the way machine learning systems and software development projects are designed, developed, and maintained, paving the way for more adaptable, efficient, and scalable solutions. By continuing to develop and refine the XaaM vision, we hope to contribute to the effective development of production-grade machine learning applications.

Acknowledgements. This research has been sponsored by NWO C2D and TKI HTSM Ecida Project Grant No. 628011003.

References

1. Arpteg, A., Brinne, B., Crnkovic-Friis, L., Bosch, J.: Software engineering challenges of deep learning. In: 2018 44th euromicro Conference on Software Engineering and Advanced Applications (SEAA), pp. 50–59. IEEE (2018)
2. Arrieta, A.B., et al.: Explainable artificial intelligence (XAI): Concepts, taxonomies, opportunities and challenges toward responsible AI. Inf. Fusion **58**, 82–115 (2020)
3. Barry, D.K., Dick, D.: Chapter 3 - web services and service-oriented architectures. In: Barry, D.K., Dick, D. (eds.) Web Services, Service-Oriented Architectures, and Cloud Computing (Second Edition), pp. 15–33. The Savvy Manager's Guides, Morgan Kaufmann, Boston (2013)

4. Baylor, D., et al.: TFX: a TensorFlow-based production-scale machine learning platform. In: Proceedings of the 23rd ACM SIGKDD International Conference on Knowledge Discovery and Data Mining, pp. 1387–1395 (2017)
5. Bisong, E., Bisong, E.: Kubeflow and kubeflow pipelines. In: Building Machine Learning and Deep Learning Models on Google Cloud Platform: A Comprehensive Guide for Beginners, pp. 671–685 (2019)
6. Bodor, A., Hnida, M., Najima, D.: MLOps: overview of current state and future directions. In: Innovations in Smart Cities Applications Volume 6: The Proceedings of the 7th International Conference on Smart City Applications, pp. 156–165. Springer (2023). https://doi.org/10.1007/978-3-031-26852-6_14
7. Briese, C., Schlüter, M., Lehr, J., Maurer, K., Krüger, J.: Towards deep learning in industrial applications taking advantage of service-oriented architectures. Procedia Manuf. **43**, 503–510 (2020)
8. Burns, B., Beda, J., Hightower, K., Evenson, L.: Kubernetes: up and running. O'Reilly Media, Inc. (2022)
9. Cao, L.: Beyond AutoML: mindful and actionable AI and AutoAI with mind and action. IEEE Intell. Syst. **37**(5), 6–18 (2022)
10. Chaudhary, A., Choudhary, C., Gupta, M.K., Lal, C., Badal, T.: Microservices in Big Data Analytics: Second International, ICETCE 2019, Rajasthan, India, February 1st-2nd 2019. Revised Selected Papers, Springer Nature (2019). https://doi.org/10.1007/978-981-15-0128-9
11. Ding, Z., Wang, S., Pan, M.: QoS-constrained service selection for networked microservices. IEEE Access **8**, 39285–39299 (2020)
12. Dobies, J., Wood, J.: Kubernetes operators: automating the container orchestration platform. O'Reilly Media (2020)
13. Dragoni, N., et al.: Microservices: yesterday, today, and tomorrow. Present Ulterior Softw. Eng., 195–216 (2017)
14. Elshawi, R., Maher, M., Sakr, S.: Automated machine learning: state-of-the-art and open challenges. arXiv preprint arXiv:1906.02287 (2019)
15. Fantinato, M., Peres, S.M., Kafeza, E., Chiu, D.K., Hung, P.C.: A review on the integration of deep learning and service-oriented architecture. J. Database Manage. (JDM) **32**(3), 95–119 (2021)
16. Garriga, M., et al.: A structural-semantic web service selection approach to improve retrievability of web services. Inf. Syst. Front. **20**, 1319–1344 (2018)
17. Gluzmann, P., Panigo, D.: Global search regression: a new automatic model-selection technique for cross-section, time-series, and panel-data regressions. Stand Genomic Sci. **15**(2), 325–349 (2015)
18. Granlund, T., Kopponen, A., Stirbu, V., Myllyaho, L., Mikkonen, T.: MLOps challenges in multi-organization setup: Experiences from two real-world cases. In: 2021 IEEE/ACM 1st Workshop on AI Engineering - Software Engineering for AI (WAIN), pp. 82–88 (2021)
19. He, X., Zhao, K., Chu, X.: AutoML: a survey of the state-of-the-art. Knowl.-Based Syst. **212**, 106622 (2021)
20. Idowu, S., Strüber, D., Berger, T.: Asset management in machine learning: state-of-research and state-of-practice. ACM Comput. Surv. **55**(7), 1–35 (2022)
21. Isdahl, R., Gundersen, O.E.: Out-of-the-box reproducibility: a survey of machine learning platforms. In: 2019 15th International Conference on eScience (eScience), pp. 86–95. IEEE (2019)
22. Kavikondala, A., Muppalla, V., Krishna Prakasha, K., Acharya, V.: Automated retraining of machine learning models. Int. J. Innov. Technol. Explor. Eng. **8**(12), 445–452 (2019)

23. Kim, G., Humble, J., Debois, P., Willis, J., Forsgren, N.: The DevOps handbook: how to create world-class agility, reliability, & security in technology organizations. IT Revolution (2021)
24. Klaise, J., Van Looveren, A., Cox, C., Vacanti, G., Coca, A.: Monitoring and explainability of models in production. arXiv preprint arXiv:2007.06299 (2020)
25. Kreuzberger, D., Kühl, N., Hirschl, S.: Machine Learning Operations (MLOps): overview, definition, and architecture. IEEE Access **11**, 31866–31879 (2023)
26. Leite, L., Rocha, C., Kon, F., Milojicic, D., Meirelles, P.: A survey of devops concepts and challenges. ACM Comput. Surv. **52**(6) (2019)
27. Li, D., Ye, D., Gao, N., Wang, S.: Service selection with QoS correlations in distributed service-based systems. IEEE Access **7**, 88718–88732 (2019)
28. Mboweni, T., Masombuka, T., Dongmo, C.: A systematic review of machine learning devops. In: 2022 International Conference on Electrical, Computer and Energy Technologies (ICECET), pp. 1–6. IEEE (2022)
29. Mäkinen, S., Skogström, H., Laaksonen, E., Mikkonen, T.: Who needs MLOps: what data scientists seek to accomplish and how can MLOps help? In: 2021 IEEE/ACM 1st Workshop on AI Engineering - Software Engineering for AI (WAIN), pp. 109–112 (2021)
30. Newman, S.: Building Microservices. O'Reilly Media, Inc. (2021)
31. Papazoglou, M.P.: Service-oriented computing: Concepts, characteristics and directions. In: Proceedings of the Fourth International Conference on Web Information Systems Engineering, 2003. WISE 2003, pp. 3–12. IEEE (2003)
32. Polyzotis, N., Roy, S., Whang, S.E., Zinkevich, M.: Data management challenges in production machine learning. In: Proceedings of the 2017 ACM International Conference on Management of Data, pp. 1723–1726 (2017)
33. Rabbani, I.M., Aslam, M., Enriquez, A.M.M., Qudeer, Z.: Service association factor (SAF) for cloud service selection and recommendation. Inf. Technol. Control **49**(1), 113–126 (2020)
34. Raschka, S., Mirjalili, V.: Python machine learning: machine learning and deep learning with Python, scikit-learn, and TensorFlow 2. Packt Publishing Ltd (2019)
35. Ravetz, J.R.: The science of 'what-if?'. Futures **29**(6), 533–539 (1997)
36. Riccio, V., Jahangirova, G., Stocco, A., Humbatova, N., Weiss, M., Tonella, P.: Testing machine learning based systems: a systematic mapping. Empir. Softw. Eng. **25**, 5193–5254 (2020)
37. Ruf, P., Madan, M., Reich, C., Ould-Abdeslam, D.: Demystifying MLOps and presenting a recipe for the selection of open-source tools. Appl. Sci. **11**(19), 8861 (2021)
38. Saltelli, A., et al.: Global sensitivity analysis: the primer. John Wiley & Sons (2008)
39. Sculley, D., et al.: Hidden technical debt in machine learning systems. In: Advances in Neural Information Processing Systems 28 (2015)
40. Symeonidis, G., Nerantzis, E., Kazakis, A., Papakostas, G.A.: MLOps - definitions, tools and challenges. In: 2022 IEEE 12th Annual Computing and Communication Workshop and Conference (CCWC), pp. 0453–0460 (2022)
41. Testi, M., et al.: MLOps: a taxonomy and a methodology. IEEE Access **10**, 63606–63618 (2022)
42. Wachter, S., Mittelstadt, B., Russell, C.: Counterfactual explanations without opening the black box: automated decisions and the GDPR. Harv. JL Tech. **31**, 841 (2017)
43. Zaharia, M., et al.: Accelerating the machine learning lifecycle with MLflow. IEEE Data Eng. Bull. **41**(4), 39–45 (2018)

44. Zhou, Y., Yu, Y., Ding, B.: Towards MLOps: a case study of ml pipeline platform. In: 2020 International Conference on Artificial Intelligence and Computer Engineering (ICAICE), pp. 494–500 (2020)
45. Zolkifli, N.N., Ngah, A., Deraman, A.: Version control system: a review. In: Procedia Computer Science, the 3rd International Conference on Computer Science and Computational Intelligence (ICCSCI 2018): Empowering Smart Technology in Digital Era for a Better Life, vol. 135, pp. 408–415 (2018)

Using the Client Cache for Content Encoding: Shared Dictionary Compression for the Web

Benjamin Wollmer[1,3]([✉]) [ID], Wolfram Wingerath[2] [ID], Felix Gessert[3] [ID],
Florian Bücklers[3], Hannes Kuhlmann[3], Erik Witt[3], Fabian Panse[1] [ID],
and Norbert Ritter[1] [ID]

[1] University of Hamburg, Hamburg, Germany
{benjamin.wollmer,fabian.panse,norbert.ritter}@uni-hamburg.de
[2] University of Oldenburg, Oldenburg, Germany
wolfram.wingerath@uni-oldenburg.de
[3] Baqend GmbH, Hamburg, Germany
{fg,bw}@baqend.com

Abstract. As different approaches have demonstrated in the past, delta encoding and shared dictionary compression can significantly reduce the payload of websites. However, choosing a good dictionary or delta source is still a challenge and has kept delta encoding from becoming practically relevant for today's web. In this work, we demonstrate that the often prohibitive costs of dictionary generation exhibited by earlier approaches can be avoided by simply using cache entries for content encoding: We divide web pages into different page types and use one actual page of every type as a dictionary to encode pages of the same type. In an experimental evaluation, we show that our approach outperforms current industry standards by a factor of 5 in terms of compression ratio. We discuss optimization and content normalization strategies as well as application scenarios that are possible with our approach, but infeasible with the current state of the art.

Keywords: Delta Encoding · Web · Shared Dictionary Compression

1 Introduction

Delta encoding is a compression method that reduces the size of a file by only describing it as a delta (i.e., relative change) with respect to another file using a dictionary that contains shared content. Our previous work shows how much data can be saved when compressing web pages by finding the optimal dictionary in the client cache and using it to calculate the delta dynamically [12,13]. However, using the smallest delta for every individual user and file is not feasible in practice because of huge computational costs and a reduced cache hit rate on

© The Author(s), under exclusive license to Springer Nature Switzerland AG 2023
M. Aiello et al. (Eds.): SummerSOC 2023, CCIS 1847, pp. 45–55, 2023.
https://doi.org/10.1007/978-3-031-45728-9_3

the CDN level[1]. Furthermore, client and server communication would suffer by negotiating what the client cache offers. Current approaches therefore use synthetic dictionaries that are created apriori and have to be made known to client and server in advance; for example, Brotli [1] compression uses a shared dictionary that is part of every major browser distribution and contains generic tokens from web content. Approaches to use custom dictionaries for individual websites have been implemented [2,4], but ultimately failed because of the high complexity and computational costs of regenerating and redistributing new dictionaries after website deployments [7].

In this work, we show how the process of choosing dictionaries can be simplified to a degree that allows it to happen at transmission time, while still maintaining a compression ratio comparable to today's static approaches. Instead of creating a synthetic dictionary or finding the smallest delta possible, we map every web page (i.e., file) to exactly one similar existing page as a dictionary. Dictionaries in our approach are thus predefined and therefore require neither costly computation nor negotiation when requesting new content. This opens up various possibilities for improving infrastructure efficiency and user-perceived performance in the web.

We make the following contributions:

C_1 *Simplification of Dictionary Selection*
After discussing related work in Sect. 2, we show how the selection of a dictionary can be simplified by simply choosing a random page from a set of the same page type.

C_2 *Evaluation with Real-World Data*
While shared dictionary compression is not available in any browser yet, we use real-world data of Speed Kit's caching architecture in Sect. 3 to calculate the expected impact of our approach on the compression ratio.

C_3 *Practical Considerations & Open Challenges*
In Sect. 4, we discuss how the complexity of shared dictionary compression can be encapsulated in a CDN-like infrastructure to make our approach available as a plugin to existing websites. We also present lines of future research to enable instant page load times through extensions of our work, such as predictive preloading of web content or transformations of the dictionary files to effectively turn them into generic templates (akin to app shells known from progressive web apps).

2   Related Work

Delta Encoding describes a file as a sequence of copy and delete instructions to build it from another file. While no implementation is used in major web browsers today, there have been efforts to include delta encoding in the HTTP

---

[1] Content delivery networks (CDNs) accelerate content delivery by caching resources that are requested by multiple clients [6]. This is obviously not possible for deltas, if they are computed for individual users.

standard by Mogul et al. [5]. While they showed that calculating the delta from an old version to a new one can significantly reduce the payload, they did not consider deltas between different files or a shared dictionary. VCDIFF, one of the most prominent differentiation algorithms, was proposed by Korn et al., as well as the name for the format of said algorithm [3]. There exists an open-source implementation by Google[2].

Shared Dictionary Compression algorithms use a dictionary for multiple files instead of a dedicated dictionary for each file. Zsdt [2] or FemtoZip[3] can be used with a shared dictionary, but they have yet to be used for web content. Currently, the only exception in the context of the web is Brotli. Despite the other approaches, Brotli uses a static dictionary known to the encoder and decoder [1]. As a result, the dictionary does not need to be transferred. While Brotli is currently the only supported shared dictionary algorithm for all major browsers, its custom dictionary capabilities are currently unavailable in all major implementations. However, there are attempts to bring shared dictionary compression with Brotli to the major web browsers [9]. All of the above mentioned shared dictionary compressors are able to train a custom dictionary from a set of given files. Shared Dictionary Compression over HTTP (SDCH) was developed by Google [4]. The basic idea was to push dictionaries to the browser so that the browser could use those to calculate the delta with VCDIFF to newly requested files. While this feature was available in Chrome, it did not get well adapted by the community: There are reports from LinkedIn claiming they could reduce their payload by up to 81% for certain files [7], but they also stated that the dictionary calculation took longer than their release cycles. Due to the low adoption, SDCH was eventually unshipped [8].

Speed Kit is an architecture developed by Baqend that enables caching dynamic content (e.g., HTML files) and various other performance optimizations for websites [10] as well as an extensive real-user monitoring (RUM), processing more than 650 million page loads every month [11]. We use Speed Kit's RUM data for our evaluation and discuss opportunities for implementing our approach in the Speed Kit architecture in Sect. 4.

3 Selecting Raw Files as Dictionaries

Training a dictionary for shared dictionary compression usually involves an algorithm that analyzes hundreds of files to be compressed with the dictionary to be trained. The main goal is to find common strings (or byte arrays) across different files and to extract them into the dictionary. Web pages are especially well-suited for this kind of compression as they typically share many common strings like div tags or CSS selectors. Also, websites often contain repeating elements which are present on almost every page, such as the navigation header, the logo, search components, or the footer. Pages on a website can further often be categorized by their page type that subsumes a set of pages with the same purpose. Web

---

[2] https://github.com/google/open-vcdiff.
[3] https://github.com/gtoubassi/femtozip.

analytics tools like Google Analytics[4] routinely distinguish pages by their type, so that our approach can use the page type information without any overhead as it is readily available in virtually any production environment[5]. For example, e-commerce websites typically define at least the product and listing page types. While a page of type product describes a product on the website, a page of type listing aggregates products of the same category. These pages are often generated with templates on the server side, like handlebars[6] or twig[7], and therefore share a lot of markup code by design. Transferring these repeating parts with every request is still the standard for server-side rendering. We argue that these similarities are sufficient to use pages[8] of the same page type as a dictionary. This has the additional benefit, that we can just use a visited page as a dictionary, without the need of transferring an actual dictionary.

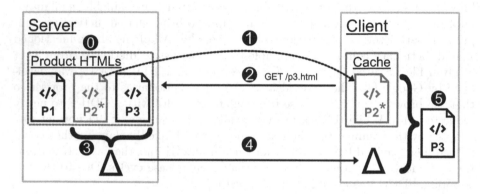

Fig. 1. The server marks one regular HTML of every page type as a dictionary(*). If a client has already seen this HTML (P2), it can now use it as a dictionary to only request small deltas to the requested file (P3), instead of the whole file.

Figure 1 shows the general idea of our approach. The server chooses one dictionary for every page type (product in this case) and tags it (*product 2* here) (**Step 0**). This can be precomputed once and then be used by every request. Note that this dictionary is just a regular HTML, but with a tag (e.g. HTTP header) to mark it as a dictionary. Each website would have as much dictionaries as it has page types and the dictionaries are not client specific, since every user will use the same set of dictionaries. As a result the server would only handle a couple of dictionaries. In the depicted case, the client cache already has the

---

[4] https://analytics.google.com/analytics/web/provision.
[5] The categorization within those page types is implemented by the website owner, e.g. by URL regex.
[6] https://handlebarsjs.com/.
[7] https://twig.symfony.com/.
[8] We only use pages within the same website as a dictionary, since browsers would prohibit sharing content across different domains.

dictionary (**Step 1**), this can happen through preloading or by regularly visiting the page (c.f. Section 4.1). The client then requests *product 3*, indicating it has *product 2* in its cache (**Step 2**). The server computes the delta between *product 2* (the dictionary) and *product 3* (**Step 3**) and sends it to the client (**Step 4**). The client then applies the delta to *product 2* and receives *product 3* (**Step 5**).

3.1   Evaluation

As of today, no major browser distribution supports shared dictionary algorithms with custom dictionaries. Therefore, we evaluated the expected benefits of this approach by compressing real-world HTML files and leave tests using browser implementations as a task for future work, to be conducted after release of the required browser features. We used Brotli as the compressor, since there are efforts to make Brotli's custom dictionaries available within web browsers (cf. Section 2). As we also have shown in our previous papers [12,13], Brotli can achieve the highest compression ratio for shared dictionary compression and also excels in decompression speed [1]. We measured our approach's compression and decompression time with Brotli on levels 6 and 11. Level 6 is essential since it is the default level used for dynamic content. Level 11 can be used for static content, which usually results in better compression ratios but a worse compression time. The hardware we used in this experiment consists of a Ryzen 5950x, 64 GB 3600 MHz RAM and a PCI 4.0 SSD to measure the timings.

The dataset is provided by Speed Kit and contains HTML files of the most requested files of the last three days for six different websites. These are all e-commerce platforms. We used the two most common page types for this work: listing and product. We fetched a total of 1420 samples of the most requested HTML pages, evenly distributed across all pages and pages types. For each page type and website combination, we used every page as a dictionary for all other pages of the same page type.

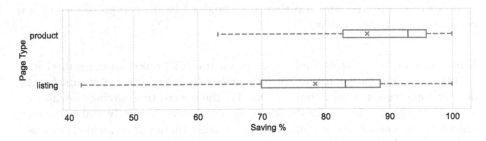

Fig. 2. Comparing the page-type dictionary to Brotli's default dictionary shows that our approach can save around 88% of transferred data.

Size. Figure 2 shows how the data saving is distributed across the different page types. We chose compression level 11 to show the best possible output, and as shown, we could reduce the payload by 88% of Brotli compression with the standard dictionary – the mean size of those deltas where in the range of 9 kB. As a comparison, the maximum *TCP* package size is 64 kB. The files can be small enough to fit into the initial congestion window, which might improve the download performance. The relative results for Brotli on level 6 look similar and are left out because of space restrictions.

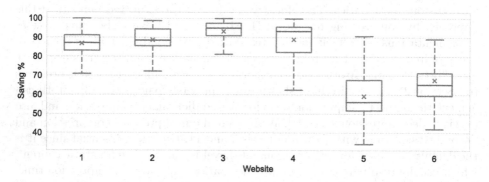

Fig. 3. Generally, all analyzed websites benefit from the page-type dictionary; some pages can save up to 93% of the size achieved by Brotli's default.

The compression ratio was relatively stable within each website. Figure 3 shows the compression ratio for each website. The first four websites where able to save more than 90% of the data, compared to Brotli's default dictionary. Website 3 performed exceptionally well, with a median saving of 93% of Brotli size with its standard dictionary. Furthermore, while websites 5 and 6 did not perform as well as the first four, they were still far ahead of the standard Brotli compression. There was also no case where the dictionary approach suffered from a worse compression ratio than the standard Brotli compression and is a considerably safe alternative.

Performance. As Fig. 4a indicates, the custom dictionary also resulted in a slightly faster compression time for most pages. This was less significant for the default compression level 6, but on level 11, there were time savings for up to a second. As Fig. 4b shows, the decompression time was generally stable through different compression levels. But since the smaller dictionaries resulted in fewer instructions, there was also a slight but negligible improvement (<3 ms).

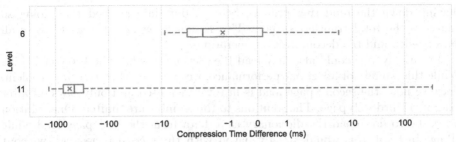

(a) The high compression level benefits the most of the custom dictionary and, in most cases, saves hundreds of milliseconds.

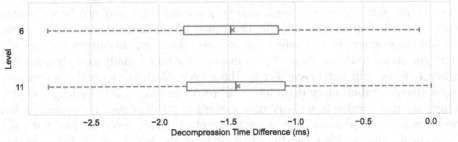

(b) Decompressing is generally fast, and the provided uplift is neglectable.

Fig. 4. Comparing the absolute difference using the custom dictionary to the standard Brotli dictionary shows that the custom dictionary, almost in all cases, outperforms the standard general purpose dictionary.

4 Practical Considerations

Using page-type dictionaries is feasible in practice. However, there are still some practical considerations.

4.1 Downloading the Dictionary

As with every shared dictionary approach, this approach only works with a given dictionary. Therefore, we cannot optimize the first-page load. But when should we download the dictionary? A naïve approach would be to split the first load of a journey[9] into the dictionary and the delta and then download them simultaneously. This approach has two critical problems: First, we introduce a dependency within the critical rendering path. Normally, the browser can read the HTML as a stream and start its work after receiving the first chunks, e.g., to resolve dependencies. While the decompression is streamable, it can only be started if the dictionary is available. The dictionary itself is likely to be bigger than the actual compressed file. As a result, the compressed file has to wait for the dictionary, and we are essentially disabling the streaming process and therefore

---

[9] A journey describes multiple consecutive page visits of one user.

slowing down the rendering process. Second, our data showed that doing so increases the total transferred data. This is unsurprising since we transfer all data needed and the decompression operations.

Intuitively, one could also lazy load the dictionary while the browser is idle. While this would not affect our performance, we still only shift the size problem. Because now, the second page load is in total increased and only pays off after loading a third web page. The solutions to this gamble are limited. One solution would be to download the dictionary as a delta from the first page load while idling. In total, this would already payoff with the second page load, without affecting the performance of the first page load. The drawback is that the server cannot precompute this delta since the users can use every page as an entry to the website (e.g., through a google search or a link). This may not be a problem since the calculation is usually in the range of milliseconds and is not time critical because we are preloading this request. However, this approach will only work for static content. Because personalized content usually gets dynamically generated and will not be cached by the server. Caching it on the server side to compute the dictionary delta later will result in some kind of sticky sessions, which are unfavorable in a distributed system due to scalability reasons. So far, we have only talked about new users to a website. This problem does not exist for returning users. They can fully benefit from the first page load of a session and, as described in Sect. 3, are likely to shrink the whole amount of HTML bytes to the size of one HTML file. Of course, longer sessions benefit even more from this approach.

4.2   Creating Template Dictionaries

Since server rendered pages are built on templates (cf. Section 3), one could also use this property by simply rendering an "empty" page and using it as the dictionary for this page type. A product page could be rendered without any product information. This template should still be a valid HTML file to be renderable. The dictionary can then act as a proxy once a page of this type is requested. Like single-page applications, the browser can render this proxy template while the actual delta is requested. Dynamically replacing the rendered template has some caveats, like double javascript execution, and may need adjustment, as described in [10], but could improve user-perceived performance. And while there are algorithms to find common strings in a set of files (cf. Section 2: femtozip, zstd), to the best of our knowledge, there is currently no algorithm available to extract a valid HTML subset of a set of given HTML files. While developers could extract said template by modifying their template engine, this approach would not be feasible from a delta infrastructure on top of existing systems. To make delta encoding feasible, this needs to be resolved. To test this approach, one could choose the most straightforward way imaginable: Just opening a random HTML file of a page type for a specific website and removing content that is specific to this page and may change for another one, making sure that we still end up with a valid HTML file. Since no specific domain knowledge is needed and the page types are typically limited, this process could quickly be done. However, more research for a templating algorithm is needed to automate and scale this templating approach.

However, by deleting the text, the content collapses and will increase in size as soon as the text of the delta arrives. This is generally poorly received by users and should be avoided. Therefore, one can change the template generation process from deleting the content to hiding it via the CSS attribute *visibility='hidden'*. The increase in file size of the additional CSS attribute is neglectable since these additions are just a few bytes after compression. Since this template still has the content, it can again be used as a preloaded HTML and instantly be rendered.

4.3 Dictionary Transitions

As described in Sect. 3, most pages share the same header and footer. And even though the main content does not share many similarities, compressing one page type dictionary to another generally results in reasonable compression ratios. This indicates that the other dictionaries can be easily derived after the browser is populated with an arbitrary dictionary. Therefore, it can also improve performance for the first page of an unseen page type. The same also applies to updating deprecated dictionaries to the newest version. Since the dictionaries are regular HTML files, they are invalidated using Speed Kit's approach [10]. If a deprecated dictionary is being used, the server can always just fallback to a regular, non-delta response.

4.4 Predictive Preloading

Preload prediction determines which pages a user will likely navigate soon and download them beforehand so that they are already available in the cache. The page can then be instantly served from the cache without downloading it again. This plays well with page-type dictionaries. While using a page-type dictionary for compression entirely discards the dictionary calculation process, it also serves as an actual page and is, therefore, present in the browser cache. With preload prediction data, this dictionary can be chosen wisely to increase the cache hit rate. Alternatively, one could use a highly frequented page, like a product advertised on the home page.

4.5 Shared Dictionary Compression at Scale

As shown in Sect. 3, we can save 88% of the HTML payload. Applying these numbers to the statistics provided by Similar Web[10], this approach could save 700 TB a month, just for the top 50 e-commerce websites. But shared dictionary compression failed in the past due to its high complexity and slow adoption. Adopting shared dictionary compression on an architecture like the one provided by Speed Kit can eliminate this complexity for website providers and make shared dictionary compression available as a plugin. Of course, this is also of

---

[10] https://www.similarweb.com/top-websites/e-commerce-and-shopping/.

interest to the user. According to Similar Web, an average user journey consists of 7.5 page loads. Depending on the website, this approach could download the whole journey of HTML files for the byte "price" of one HTML (cf. Section 3.1).

5 Conclusion

In theory, shared dictionary compression (SDC) seems like the perfect fit for transmitting web content as it can result in significantly better compression ratios compared with today's web compression standards such as Brotli. In practice, however, SDC has yet to be adopted in a web context, because negotiating dictionaries between client and server has always turned out prohibitively complex. In this paper, we show that HTML pages from the client cache can be used as dictionaries to reduce the payload of HTML files by up to 88% for single pages, as soon as browser implementations add support for custom dictionaries with Brotli. In evaluating the compression ratio for our approach, we show that the benefit of choosing the smallest delta is negligible when comparing it to using an arbitrary file as a dictionary. We finally discuss how our approach could innovate web content delivery through mechanisms like predictive preloading of web content that are not feasible with the current state of the art.

References

1. Alakuijala, J., et al.: Brotli: a general-purpose data compressor. ACM TOI **37**(1), 1–30 (2018)
2. Collet, Y., M. Kucherawy, E.: Zstandard Compression and the 'application/zstd' Media Type. RFC 8878, February 2021
3. Korn, D., MacDonald, J., Mogul, J., Vo, K.: The VCDIFF Generic Differencing and Compression Data Format. RFC 3284, June 2002
4. McQuade, B., Mixter, K., Lee, W.H., Butler, J.: A proposal for shared dictionary compression over http (2016)
5. Mogul, J., et al.: Delta Encoding in HTTP. RFC 3229, January 2002
6. Pathan, M., Buyya, R.: A Taxonomy of CDNs, pp. 33–77. Springer, Heidelberg (2008). https://doi.org/10.1007/978-3-540-77887-5_2
7. Shapira, O.: SDCH at LinkedIn (2015). https://engineering.linkedin.com/shared-dictionary-compression-http-linkedin. Accessed Mar 2023
8. Sleevi, R.: Intent to Unship: SDCH (2016). https://groups.google.com/a/chromium.org/d/msg/blink-dev/nQl0ORHy7sw/HNpR96sqAgAJ. Accessed Mar 2023
9. Weiss, Y., Meenan, P.: Compression dictionary transport (2023). https://github.com/WICG/compression-dictionary-transport. Accessed Mar 2023
10. Wingerath, W., et al.: Speed Kit: A Polyglot & GDPR-Compliant Approach For Caching Personalized Content. In: ICDE, Dallas, Texas (2020)
11. Wingerath, W., et al.: Beaconnect: continuous web performance A/B-testing at scale. In: Proceedings of the 48th International Conference on Very Large Data Bases (2022)

12. Wollmer, B., Wingerath, W., Ferrlein, S., Panse, F., Gessert, F., Ritter, N.: The case for cross-entity delta encoding in web compression. In: Proceedings of the 22nd International Conference on Web Engineering (ICWE) (2022)
13. Wollmer, B., Wingerath, W., Ferrlein, S., Panse, F., Gessert, F., Ritter, N.: The case for cross-entity delta encoding in web compression (extended). J. Web Eng. **22**(01), 131–146 (2023)

Smart*

Privacy in Connected Vehicles: Perspectives of Drivers and Car Manufacturers

Andrea Fieschi[2], Yunxuan Li[1]([✉]), Pascal Hirmer[1], Christoph Stach[1], and Bernhard Mitschang[1]

[1] IPVS, University of Stuttgart, Stuttgart, Germany
{yunxuan.li,pascal.hirmer,christoph.stach,
bernhard.mitschang}@ipvs.uni-stuttgart.de
[2] Mercedes-Benz AG, Stuttgart, Germany
andrea.fieschi@mercedes-benz.com

Abstract. The digital revolution has led to significant technological advancements in the automotive industry, enabling vehicles to process and share information with other vehicles and the cloud. However, as data sharing becomes more prevalent, privacy protection has become an essential issue. In this paper, we explore various privacy challenges regarding different perspectives of drivers and car manufacturers. We also propose general approaches to overcome these challenges with respect to their individual needs. Finally, we highlight the importance of collaboration between drivers and car manufacturers to establish trust and achieve better privacy protection.

Keywords: Connected Vehicles · Privacy · Anonymization

1 Introduction

Connected Vehicles (CVs) are a revolutionary advancement in the field of transportation that combines traditional vehicles with modern technology to enhance their capabilities. CVs are vehicles that are equipped with modern applications (apps) and are capable of accessing the internet, collecting and processing real-time data from multiple sources, and interacting with their external environments [3]. With these capabilities, CVs have become a significant source of data extraction, providing insights into driving behavior, vehicle performance, and other valuable data points. While these vehicle data can be useful for achieving autonomous driving or providing personalized services to drivers, they also contain sensitive information that could potentially identify the driver. Hence, privacy protection has become an emerging concern in the automotive industry.

Supported by SofDCar (19S21002), which is funded by the German Federal Ministry for Economic Affairs and Climate Action, Mercedes-Benz AG, GSaME.

M. Aiello et al. (Eds.): SummerSOC 2023, CCIS 1847, pp. 59–68, 2023.
https://doi.org/10.1007/978-3-031-45728-9_4

In domains such as IoT and smartphones, privacy protection solutions are available. Nonetheless, Connected Vehicle Environments (CVEs) possess specific characteristics that need to be taken into account [16]. The solution proposed in other domains can be used as inspiration but not directly translated to the CV domain. While CVs can communicate with various entities in CVEs, such as roadside units, this paper focuses on privacy protection issues regarding data exchange between vehicles and the cloud. For instance, car manufacturers collect data in order to provide services. This data exchange and its privacy implications are at the center of attention in our discussion.

In our previous work [7], we explored the significance of privacy in CVEs, listing examples of data collection use cases, e.g., battery improvement, live traffic monitoring, and "pay how you drive" car insurance. However, stakeholders, such as individual drivers and car manufacturers, hold varying interests in privacy protection in CVEs. While drivers have a vested interest in protecting their personal information, such as location and driving habits, car manufacturers seek to improve their products through the analysis of privacy-protected data.

In this paper, we analyze the current situation, outline a first approach to overcome the discussed privacy challenges while accommodating the individual needs of both parties, and define the ground for future research. This paper explores the key privacy challenges in the CVE from the perspectives of drivers and car manufacturers, which are discussed in Sect. 2 and Sect. 3, respectively. Thus, in Sect. 4, we outline the general requirements for cooperation and building trust between drivers and car manufacturers. Finally, we summarize the paper and give an outlook on future work in Sect. 5.

2   Privacy from the Driver's Perspective

Based on domain expert discussions, we have derived a privacy attack model for CVEs from the driver's perspective. As depicted in Fig. 1, this model considers the underlying CV as *trusted-and-secure*. This implies that any personal data stored in the CV cannot be accessed or shared without the driver's consent, and all computations performed within the CV are secure and resilient to attempts to compromise them. However, remote services, such as applications whose computation is executed external to a CV, are considered as *honest-but-curious*. That is, these services comply with legal and driver-consent policies regarding the processing, storage, and sharing of personal data. Nevertheless, as drivers lost control of their personal data when sharing them with remote services, they still have concerns that remote services would derive sensitive information from the collected data.

2.1   Privacy Challenges for Drivers

Despite the desire of drivers to protect their personal data, their general demand is to continue utilizing as many user-dependent applications enabled by the CVs as possible, such as using navigation or fatigue detection services. To ensure

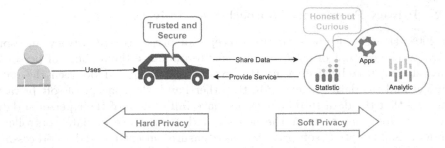

Fig. 1. Privacy Attack Model from Driver's Perspective for Car to Cloud Environment

the functionality of these services, certain vehicle data must be shared, such as location data for navigation services. Furthermore, sharing a greater quantity and higher quality of data allows the service provider to conduct more detailed analyses and, therefore, offer better customized services. However, the increased volume and precision of the data shared by drivers also pose greater privacy risks, as they may reveal sensitive information about their driving behavior and activities. Thus, a challenge of preserving privacy in CVEs is to balance the trade-off between privacy protection and service quality.

Another challenge of preserving privacy in CVEs is to achieve Situation-Awareness [11]. As the sensitivity of a data point is related to when and where as well as for what purpose the data is being collected [8], drivers' privacy requirements can also change when the situation changes. For instance, drivers may agree to share their unmodified location and speed data with a data collection company for analysis purposes when they are driving adhere to traffic regulations. However, in the occurrence of an accidental speeding violation, drivers would revise their privacy requirements to hide their speeding behavior. Hence, approaches to privacy protection in CVEs must consider the dynamic and context-dependent nature of drivers' privacy needs.

Although privacy is a highly concerning issue in many domains, users often struggle to manage their privacy settings effectively. For instance, Ramokapane et al. [13] found that many smartphone users find it difficult to customize privacy features provided by their smartphone manufacturers, as they lack knowledge on how to configure them. From our research project, we noticed that the aforementioned challenge is magnified in the automobile domain since CVs typically have significantly more data sources and potential data consumers than smartphones. Consequently, managing the fine-graind and situation-aware privacy policy for a CV can easily create information and choice overhead for drivers. As a result, the difficulties in managing privacy settings would contribute to the so-called "privacy paradox" [12], where people claim to be concerned about their privacy but still share a lot of private information.

2.2 Privacy Protection Approaches for Drivers

In 2008, Danezis [6] proposed two concepts of privacy: hard privacy and soft privacy. The concept of hard privacy aims to minimize the amount of personal data shared, thereby decreasing the level of trust required between the data subject and the data collector. On the other hand, the concept of soft privacy assumes that the data subject does not have full control of their personal data and, therefore, has to trust the honesty and competence of data controllers. Under this assumption, soft privacy aims to ensure consent-based data processing through policies, access control, and audit.

As depicted in Fig. 1, we argue that both concepts are essential in preserving privacy in CVE. The general concept is to achieve hard privacy before vehicle data leave the CV while ensuring soft privacy for data that is shared with different remote services. To achieve data minimization of hard privacy, services must provide drivers with essential metadata, such as what vehicle data are collected and for what purpose. They should also support drivers in managing their privacy policies in a fine-granular manner. Based on the assumption that services are honest-but-curious, the service's metadata is considered reliable and will be used to conduct data minimization.

In accordance with the concept of hard privacy, drivers are advised to block any unnecessary data sharing for the desired service functionality based on the information provided in the services' metadata. This would provide a basic level of privacy protection against the curious nature of different services. For the data that are necessary for the computation of the desired service, data minimization can still be achieved through different approaches, such as reducing the accuracy of the vehicle data. To balance the trade-off between privacy protection and service quality, different Privacy Enhancing Technologies (PETs) [15], such as obfuscation and pseudonymization, can be utilized to distort or anonymize vehicle data so that the sensitive information is removed and the perturbed data are still precise enough to ensure service functionality. Furthermore, there is the challenge of handling scenarios where the privacy requirements of drivers may change depending on the situation. As a result, different PETs used in CVs should be developed in a modular manner, and the data processing in CVs should also support live adaptation, allowing for the dynamic integration, replacement, or removal of PETs in the vehicle's data pipeline.

To utilize service functionalities, it is inevitable that drivers have to share certain vehicle data with the corresponding service providers. As drivers no longer have control over the shared data, we can only ensure soft privacy for them. To mitigate privacy leakage risks, a Service Level Agreement (SLA) can be established between the driver and the service provider before the driver uses the service for the first time. Through the privacy section of the SLA, the service provider should enable drivers to explicitly express how their shared data can be further processed, stored, or published. However, as drivers usually do not have insight into data processing, it is important for them to receive transparent information regarding how their data is being processed by the service provider.

Additionally, to assist drivers with a basic understanding of privacy in customizing their privacy policies for CVs and managing their privacy preferences in SLAs, user-friendly privacy management mechanisms, such as the privacy context model dedicated to CVs [10], have to be developed. Overall, by adopting the concepts of hard and soft privacy, we can strike a balance between protecting drivers' privacy while still ensuring various service functionalities.

3   Privacy from the Car Manufacturer's Perspective

From the point of view of a data-collecting company, privacy protection is important for multiple reasons. Firstly, companies have an ethical obligation to ensure privacy protection for their users, thereby adhering to ethical guidelines and minimizing the risk of privacy violations. Secondly, legal compliance is crucial, as the General Data Protection Regulation (GDPR), enforced by the European Union, mandates strict restrictions and limitations on data collection to safeguard user privacy. Lastly, the implementation of robust data protection measures can be particularly appealing to customers. Prioritizing privacy and making it a core value of a company will help gain further trust with the general public and add value to its products.

3.1   Privacy Challenges for Car Manufacturers

From a data science perspective, CVs represent an immensely valuable source of data, as they allow manufacturing companies to monitor how their products perform in real-world scenarios, gain insights into usage patterns and preferences, and identify opportunities for improvement or redevelopment in the next iteration. However, it is important to note that the data collected from these vehicles can be closely linked to the behavior of the drivers. As a result, the improper use of CVs can lead to the risk of leaking personal information, such as the position of the car, their general behavior behind the wheel, and other habits that are kept inside the vehicle. It is imperative that this information remains secure and inaccessible to unauthorized parties, and if possible not linkable to a specific person, i.e. anonymized. Drivers must have the assurance that any data they choose to share will only be used to enhance their service and experience and that none of the collected information will be used against them. Therefore, manufacturers must ensure that adequate privacy measures are in place.

With regard to privacy, data collection use cases can be mainly divided in user dependent and user independent use cases [7]. These come with different and specific privacy challenges. User dependent use cases need to collect data and send information back to the same specific user, so the data need to be protected but connected to an identifiable source. User independent use cases collect data to then provide a service to entire fleets, anonymization becomes an option with the extra challenge of guaranteeing a high level of anonymity. In Fig. 2 we have a graphical representation of these two kinds of data collection.

It should be noted that the collection of data from cars raises privacy concerns, not only for the driver but also for individuals who are merely in the vicinity of the vehicle. Camera data, for instance, may include images of pedestrians that could potentially identify them and disclose their whereabouts at a specific time. Additionally, companies must ensure that they do not collect data that goes beyond what is necessary. If a driver declines to share their identity in connection with the collected data, the data collector must ensure that the driver's identity cannot be inferred by analyzing patterns in the data.

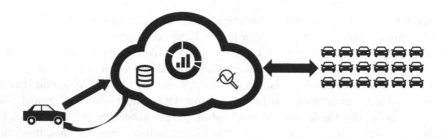

Fig. 2. Manufacturer's Perspective: Single customer-related services (left) and fleet-focused services (right)

Offering strong privacy protection policies presents several challenges and difficulties for companies. Firstly, drivers must provide consent for data collection, and the data can only be used for agreed purposes. Any further analysis of the data is prohibited. Pre-processing may be necessary on board the vehicle before data transfer, and communication channels must be secure. Another challenge is the inability to use data retrospectively for unforeseen purposes, requiring new data collection campaigns and new user agreements.

3.2   Privacy Protection Approaches for Car Manufacturers

If a privacy-conscious company wishes to provide even stronger protection, additional computational and design efforts are required. Changing data collection campaigns, such as incorporating new data types to be gathered, may necessitate redesigning and new user agreements have to be stipulated with the driver, which can prolong the time needed to provide data to analysts. A significant challenge is information loss, as data privacy often comes at the cost of sacrificing some information that raw data would convey. The trade-off between privacy protection and information content requires consideration, as stronger protection may necessitate relinquishing additional data.

This shows that privacy is not an element that can simply be added in hindsight as a plug-in element to the data flow chain. Privacy needs to be taken into account during the development of the data collection use case, every privacy methodology should fit in a frame of privacy by the design. From the early stage of design the developer should take into account the importance of privacy and it's implications. Important elements to consider are: the data type needed for the service and how they could be used to violate the users privacy; which amount of information loss will occur with different PETs; how the data collection could be structured differently in order to have a better ratio of quality of service and privacy protection.

A privacy-conscious car manufacturer models its data acquisition scenarios after various privacy-preserving methodologies to protect individual privacy. These methodologies include differential privacy [5], which involves perturbing the data to achieve privacy protection; federated learning [9], which processes the data on-board and collaboratively trains networks; homomorphic encryption [2], which protects the data during processing without decrypting the information; and k-anonymization [14], which groups data-points into equivalence classes of size k in order to protect the individual's identity. Each of these privacy-preserving approaches requires adaptation of the data collection scenario to meet their respective paradigms. Companies can gain enhanced user trust and competitive advantage by guaranteeing strong privacy policies. The trusted status of the company can encourage users to share more data, resulting in added value for the company, subsequently resulting in new and improved products for the customers. In summary, companies offering strong privacy protection policies must overcome numerous challenges and obstacles. However, the advantages of gaining user trust and enhanced value outweigh the challenges. Companies can achieve this by implementing robust security measures, ensuring transparency, obtaining user consent, and complying with relevant privacy regulations.

4   Discussion

Privacy protection in CVEs is a complex task, as the perspectives of drivers and car manufacturers may differ. From a driver's point of view, preserving the privacy of their personal data refers to balancing privacy protection and service quality in their privacy policies. Additionally, the dynamic and context-dependent nature of drivers' privacy needs must also be recognized. To overcome these challenges, we proposed a first approach in this paper, which ensures drivers' privacy by utilizing various PETs to achieve hard privacy before any vehicle data leave the CV and to ensure soft privacy through SLAs for data that is shared with different remote services.

However, achieving this goal requires the collaboration of remote service providers and car manufacturers. Primarily, remote services must be transparent about the data they collect and the purpose for which it will be used. Additionally, both service providers and car manufacturers should give drivers the freedom to customize their privacy preferences in a precise manner, which may include refusing requests for unnecessary vehicle data or reducing the quality of data that is necessary for the desired service functionality. In return, drivers must understand that these actions may result in a reduction in service quality.

From the car manufacturer's perspective, there is a strong interest in making privacy protection a priority and a key value of their company. That comes at their advantage since it also fulfills an ethical obligation and a legal compliance requirement to protect users' privacy. Collecting vehicles' data comes with a variegated constellation of challenges: providing high-performing services without collecting more data than necessary, implementing a privacy-preserving structure that allows guaranteeing strong privacy protection, gaining the trust of the drivers, and having them agree to share informative data about their cars.

A transparent data handling from the manufacturer needs to be matched with users willing to express their privacy requirements and understand the risks of agreeing to share data. Understanding that a very low amount of information will not allow the service to be top-notch but guarantee a stronger level of privacy is also a concept that the driver needs to understand fully; this should by any means come with the implication that top-notch services cannot guarantee privacy protection though, that always needs to be a priority. Drivers that communicate privacy preferences and well-thought-out boundaries are of highly valuable worth to a privacy-conscious car manufacturer.

Privacy protection in CVEs is not a one-sided issue. While implementing excessive PETs within CVs would compromise data quality of shared data, the scarcity of privacy protections within CVs also shifts greater responsibility to car manufacturers to meet the driver's privacy requirements. Thus, PETs used in CVs must be chosen carefully to enable privacy protection while ensuring sufficient data quality. However, there are still limited PETs available that are designed specifically for the privacy protection of CVs. To tackle this challenge, privacy mechanisms from other domains could be adapted in CVEs. For instance, the PRIVACY-AWARE concept proposed by Alpers et al. [1] for mobile devices, or the state-of-the-art PETs summarized by Curzon et al. [4] for smart cities. Nevertheless, there is still room for developing new PETs dedicated to CVs that can guarantee privacy without compromising service quality.

Car manufacturers and drivers have various challenges to overcome, various sets of requirements they need to evaluate, and the common goal of safeguarding people's privacy. Cooperation between the two parties and efficient as well as open communication about this topic is the way to be taken to improve privacy while still allowing services to become more sophisticated. In the meantime, laws and regulations governing the collection and processing of personal data should be enhanced and improved regularly to keep pace with technological advancements. With an infrastructure that allows drivers to fully express their privacy preferences without burdening them with a cumbersome task, and with transparent data handling from the data collectors' side, the potential for enhanced privacy protection and improved service performance can be greatly increased.

5   Summary and Future Work

In conclusion, privacy is a crucial factor to consider for both car manufacturers and drivers. While car manufacturers need to implement robust privacy measures to protect sensitive data collected from vehicles, drivers need to be aware of their privacy rights and take steps to safeguard their personal information. Failure to prioritize privacy can lead to severe consequences such as data breaches or loss of trust between manufacturers and customers. Therefore, it is imperative for all stakeholders to recognize the importance of privacy in the automotive industry and take appropriate measures to ensure that privacy is protected.

To better understand how car manufacturers can cooperate with drivers regarding privacy protection, we plan to conduct a user study to comprehend drivers' privacy awareness and requirements in CVEs as well as interviews with domain experts to gain insights into manufacturers' strategies and legal constraints. Furthermore, we also plan to research existing PETs specifically designed for CVEs as well as PETs utilized in other relevant domains to assess the feasibility and potential applicability of these technologies in the CVEs. This would help us identify suitable PETs for CVs that can guarantee privacy protection without compromising service quality. Overall, our research will further explore the effective approaches and mechanisms that facilitate collaboration in privacy protection between car manufacturers and drivers in CVEs.

References

1. Alpers, S., et al.: PRIVACY-AVARE: an approach to manage and distribute privacy settings. In: ICCC'17, pp. 1460–1468 (2017)
2. Armknecht, F., et al.: A guide to fully homomorphic encryption. In: IACR Cryptol. ePrint Arch., p. 1192 (2015)
3. Coppola, R., Morisio, M.: Connected Car: technologies, issues, future trends. ACM Comput. Surv. **49**(3), 1–36 (2016)
4. Curzon, J., et al.: A survey of privacy enhancing technologies for smart cities. Pervasive Mobile Comput. **55**, 76–95 (2019)
5. Cynthia, D., Aaron, R.: The algorithmic foundations of differential privacy.In: Found. Trends Theor. Comput. Sci. 9.3-4, 211–407 (2014)
6. Danezis, G.: Talk: introduction to privacy technology (2007). http://www0.cs.ucl.ac.uk/staff/G.Danezis/talks/Privacy_Technology_cosic.pdf
7. Fieschi, A., et al.: Anonymization use cases for data transfer in the automotive domain. In: PerCom-PerVehicle'23, pp. 98–103 (2023)
8. Gharib, M., et al.: An ontology for privacy requirements via a systematic literature review. J. Data Semant. **9**(4), 123–149 (2020)
9. Konečný, J., et al.: Federated optimization: distributed optimization beyond the datacenter. In: CoRR abs/1511.03575 (2015)
10. Li, Y., et al.: CV-Priv: towards a context model for privacy policy creation for CVs. In: PerCom-CoMoRea'23, pp. 583–588 (2023)
11. Li, Y., et al.: Ensuring situation-aware privacy for connected vehicles. In: IoT'22. Association for Computing Machinery, pp. 135–138 (2023)
12. Norberg, P., et al.: The privacy paradox: personal information disclosure intentions versus behaviors. J. Consum. Aff. **41**(1), 100–126 (2007)
13. Ramokapane, K.M., et al.: Skip, Skip, Skip, Accept!!!: a study on the usability of smartphone manufacturer provided default features and user privacy. In: PoPETs 2019.2, pp. 209–227 (2019)
14. Samarati, P., et al.: Generalizing data to provide anonymity when disclosing information (Abstract). In: PODS'98. ACM Press (1998)

15. Van Blarkom, G., et al.: Handbook of privacy and privacy-enhancing technologies. In: PISA Consortium, The Hague 198, p. 14 (2003)
16. Wang, H., et al.: Architectural design alternatives based on cloud/edge/fog computing for connected vehicles. IEEE Commun. Surv. Tutor. **22**(4), 2349–2377 (2020)

Services in Smart Manufacturing: Comparing Automated Reasoning Techniques for Composition and Orchestration

Flavia Monti, Luciana Silo, Francesco Leotta$^{(\boxtimes)}$, and Massimo Mecella

Sapienza Università di Roma, Rome, Italy
{monti,silo,leotta,mecella}@diag.uniroma1.it

Abstract. In recent years, there has been an increase interest in using intelligent methods to control manufacturing processes. Tens of resources to be modeled and offered as services through Industrial APIs, may be used in these processes and orchestrated throughout the various supply chain companies. The orchestration must be flexible and adaptable to disruption since the status of the various services/resources changes over time in terms of their cost, quality, and likelihood of failure. Due to the large amount of services involved and the complexity of their behaviors, manually making judgments quickly becomes impractical, necessitating the use of automated solutions to resolve the issue. By relying on the resources information provided by proper Industrial APIs, we can make current supply chains flexible and robust. In this work, we investigate the potential and limitations of automated reasoning techniques to enable adaptivity and resilience in smart manufacturing.

Keywords: Industrial APIs · Smart manufacturing · Automated reasoning

1 Introduction

The concept of *smart manufacturing*, commonly also mentioned as *Industry 4.0*, embodies a vision of industrial processes where computing devices are integrated in most of the manufacturing steps. In particular, industrial processes are supposed to be fully (or mostly) automated, adaptive to changes, flexible, evolvable, resilient to errors and attentive to the more knowledgeable operators' skills and needs.

Nevertheless, processes in current manufacturing landscape, must not be considered isolated. Instead, they involve several companies along intricate supply chains networks [3]. Such players co-operate together to accomplish various production goals. They consist of loosely coupled, autonomous entities with equal

---

F. Monti and L. Silo—Contributed equally.

M. Aiello et al. (Eds.): SummerSOC 2023, CCIS 1847, pp. 69–83, 2023.
https://doi.org/10.1007/978-3-031-45728-9_5

rights, and their organizational structure is dynamically adapted in accordance with the tasks to be carried out [33]. Supply Chain Design (SCD) [22] is typically a difficult job with numerous competing objectives. Facility location planning, allocation of customers to distribution centers or factories and suppliers selection are some of them. In addition, recovery strategies are a fundamental tactic for dealing with disruption events caused, for instance, by broken machines or environmental perturbation. The literature contains a variety of heading techniques [31], including relational strategies such as supply chain collaboration, communication and information exchange [6]. In this sense, it is essential for alliances to contribute to quickly recover from disruption and to collaboratively plan with other supply chain partners. Furthermore, a flexible supply chain network structure is suitable for developing effective disruption risk recovery strategies [12].

In general, a common goal in this context is the development of the *triple-A* supply chain, which consists of the simultaneous implementation of *agility* – responding to short-term changes in demand or supply quickly, *adaptability* – adjusting supply chain design to accommodate market changes, and *alignment*, establishing incentives for supply chain partners to improve performance of the entire chain [25]. We enrich such a notion by including *resilience*, as the ability to react to disruptions along the chain. It is clear that the ability of a system to adapt to certain conditions, e.g., a rescheduling of the production process, and the capacity to continue the work despite disruptions, such as the breakdown of a machine, are two crucial objectives in a smart manufacturing environment. And besides, these are particularly challenging due to the dynamism and uncertainty of manufacturing processes. As an example, machines are subject to wear and can show unpredictable behaviors, so they may often not perform their job properly.

The overall amount of manufacturing resources in the supply chain is substantial. Also, they belong to several different categories including software systems, machines, robots, and human workers. Each resource offers a specific collection of capabilities and has unique qualities, e.g., speed, costs, and probability of break. Noteworthy, the very same functionality can be offered by different resources, optionally from different categories (e.g., painting a part can be done either by a machine or by a human), and the execution of a multi-party process requires an accurate selection of resources in order to be completed in the most convenient way. Such a selection though, cannot be considered permanent as characteristics of resources change over time as well as needs and conflicting performance measures. Additionally, non-trivial constraints between resources may exist, making the overall task of choosing actions and resources difficult to be performed manually. In this regard, the employment of Artificial Intelligence (AI) techniques can simplify the task. In particular, specific automated reasoning techniques though have their own expressiveness that, in turn, influences the computational costs.

In this paper, we explore how automated reasoning techniques, which are a specific type of AI, can be used to enable adaptivity and resilience to multi-party processes in smart manufacturing. In fact, it is claimed that the use of specialized supporting technologies and techniques enable the advent of AI-augmented Business Process Management Systems (ABPMSs) [13], an emerging class of process-aware information systems empowered by trustworthy AI technology which enhance the execution of business processes with the aim of making them more adaptable, proactive, explainable, and context-sensitive. To this aim, as proposed in [5], we model the manufacturing resources as components of a Service Oriented Architecture (SOA). Each manufacturing resource involved in the supply chain is a service accessible through *Industrial Application Programming Interfaces (APIs)*. Industrial APIs provide many features like accessing the selected services, enabling quick integration, monitoring the behavior and status information, and invoking commands. In particular, with respect to the status, an Industrial APIs allows to access peculiar information about the Remaining Useful Life (RUL) of a resource, the cost, and the probability of failure, which evolves over time. We embed such an approach in a framework able to support adaptivity and propose different AI methods to assist it.

In order to show the suitability of the different approaches, we apply them to the tricky case of integrated circuits (chip) manufacturing, analyzing the efficiency, adaptivity, and limitations of the different approaches. Although semiconductor design activities are concentrated in specific regions of the USA, as well as in Europe and Japan, semiconductor manufacturing is more widely dispersed. The industries that provide manufacturing inputs and purchase finished semiconductor products are often dominated by large, multinational organizations [26]. In addition, as witnessed by the recent evolution of international political affairs, this production is strongly influenced by relationships among countries, which may produce unpredictable effects on the supply chain.

The rest of the paper is structured as follows: Sect. 2 presents a framework enabling adaptivity in smart manufacturing, while Sect. 3 presents the motivating case study we analyze. Section 4 presents the various approaches we investigate to compute a *resilient* and *adaptive* plan for industrial production. Section 5 compares and discusses the presented approaches. Finally, relevant literature and concluding remarks are presented in Sect. 6 and Sect. 7, respectively.

2   A Framework Supporting Adaptivity

We propose a service-based framework enabling adaptivity in smart manufacturing (see Fig. 1). We identify three main components, i.e., Industrial APIs, Enactor and Controller, each characterized by fundamental roles.

On the one hand, we enable interoperability between the manufacturing resources by modeling each of them as a service. The term resource encompasses here a wide range of actors including machines, humans, companies and provided services. Thus, we create a service-based supply chain consisting of a composition of services. Such services are realized as *Industrial APIs*. We consider these as APIs provided by the resources and employing specific industrial protocols (e.g., MQTT, OPC-UA) rather than classical ones (e.g., REST). The Industrial APIs are used to represent the physical actors and perfectly describe their functionalities (or tasks). They allow to monitor the behavior and status information and allow to invoke commands. The core component of the Industrial APIs is a server that allows the management of all the services involved

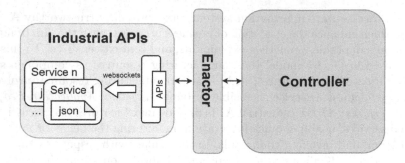

Fig. 1. A service-based adaptive framework

in the process. The server is in turn composed of a WebSocket server and an HTTP server. Particularly, it connects to the services via WebSockets in separate communication channels, and exposes a set of APIs to manage external HTTP requests. The defined APIs allow retrieving both the specification and the current state of the services and request the execution of a task to be performed by a service. Each manufacturing resource is described as a JSON file which is used by the server to "build" the service. The JSON file contains specific elements: *(i)* an *id* to specify the identifier of the service, e.g., name of the resource, *(ii)* some *attributes* that contain the static characteristics of the service, e.g., actions and costs, and *(iii)* some *features* that contains the dynamic characteristics of the service, e.g., status, breaking and quality condition. The way attributes and features are represented varies depending on the scenario in which the Industrial APIs are used.

On the other hand, the *enactor* and *controller* components are responsible both to manage and enable adaptivity in smart manufacturing. The enactor acts as a middleware by interfacing with the Industrial APIs in order to check whether the available services have changed (for instance, because of the wearing out during the execution, some services may become unavailable). The controller, which we modeled as a black box, represents the implementation of the adaptive techniques. It takes as input the specification of the involved resources (in our case a set of services) and the final target (in our case a manufacturing goal) and provides as output an adaptive orchestration[1]. Such an orchestration contains the specification of the identified services required to reach the final goal. Following the output of the controller, the enactor calls (HTTP requests through the Industrial APIs) the designed services.

By taking into account the various possibilities for the inputs and outputs of the controller, a conceptual classification of the potential strategies produced as output by the controller can be specified. We can distinguish among the deterministic and probabilistic behaviors of manufacturing resources and the complete

---

[1] In a SOA, and in this paper specifically, orchestration and process can be considered as equivalent.

and under specification of the manufacturing goals. Three distinct categories of strategies are described in the paragraphs that follow.

Instance Repair. The process behind the supply chain is well-defined. If an unexpected exception happens (e.g., a machine breaks), automated reasoning is employed in order to take the states of resources back to the expected ones. In this case, adaptivity is applied locally, but the overall forthcoming orchestration (i.e., the remaining part after the exception) remains unchanged.

Instance Planning. Every time that a new process instance is needed, automated reasoning is applied taking as input the most recent information about resources and producing as output an entire orchestration specification. If, at a certain point of the execution, something (e.g., a broken resource) prevents the plan to be completed, automated reasoning is applied again.

Policy-Based. Automated reasoning is employed to obtain a policy, i.e., a function that for each state proposes the next action. Differently from the *instance planning* case, here, if something unexpected happens, there is no need to reapply planning, as all the possibilities have been already computed.

The intuitions of three methods implementing *(i)* an instance planning approach based on deterministic services and loosely specified target, *(ii)* a policy-based approach with stochastic behaviors and fully specified target, and *(iii)* a policy-based approach with stochastic behaviors and a loosely specified target are described in Sect. 4. We are not considering any instance repair approach as we focused on the data perspective more than the control flow perspective, which is fundamental as full adaptivity requires the process structure to be very flexible. An example of a technique of this type, even if not applied in a smart manufacturing scenario but in a ubiquitous computing one, has been proposed and investigated in [30].

3 Motivating Case Study

In this section, we present the supply chain case study, i.e., *ChipChain*. It represents the chip supply chain production which involves several actors associated with different operations[2]. The main goal is the production of chips and we distinguish two main phases, the raw materials and design assortment phase, and the manufacturing process phase. The manufacturing operations involved in the *chip* supply chain are outlined below:

– *Raw materials and design assortment*: consists of the collection of the chip design (e.g., CAD model) and the essential raw materials, i.e., (silicon) wafer,

---

[2] Cf. https://www.screen.co.jp/spe/en/process and https://www.asml.com/en/news/stories/2021/semiconductor-manufacturing-process-steps.

silicon, boron, phosphor, aluminum, resistance, plastic, copper frame, and chemicals. The design and the raw materials constitute the objects involved in the *manufacturing process*.

– *Manufacturing process*: upon the assortment phase is completed, the manufacturing process begins. It represents the effective set of operations for the manufacturing of chips. Such operations include: *(i)* cleaning of the silicon wafers; *(ii)* deposition of thin film of conducting and isolating materials, e.g., silicon and aluminum; *(iii)* coating of the wafer surface with resistance; *(iv)* exposing of the wafer with ultraviolet radiation; *(v)* "development" and *(vi)* etching of the wafer; *(vii)* implantation of phosphor, boron ions or silicon; *(viii)* creation of micro transistors through a heat processing; *(ix)* stripping off of resistance (using chemicals); *(x)* separation of the wafer into individual chips connected to a copper frame; *(xi)* testing phase of the chips; and *(xii)* enclosing in plastic by leaving only the contact pins on the outside.

We based the manufacturing process in the United States (US), which is home to the vast majority of the top semiconductor suppliers in the world[3]. Additionally, we identified the list of states involved in the assortment phase. In particular, we identified the countries that produced the raw materials and considered them as the organizations part of the supply chain. In addition, we determined the costs of carrying out each operation. The distance between the US and the identified states is used to calculate them (if the object is made in the US, the associated operation cost is unitary). The *manufacturing process* is a different matter. Indeed, the manufacturing actors (machines and operators) are located in a unique factory (in the US) and the cost of the operations is set to 1. However, we take into account the possibility of more than one of the same actor performing the same action, in which case their costs are increased by a factor greater than 1.

4   Adaptive Supply Chain Approaches

In this section, we explain in detail how we implement the approaches used for finding a manufacturing production plan that ensures adaptivity in the *ChipChain* case study.

4.1   Instance Planning

Generally, by leveraging automated planning techniques, it is possible to automatically orchestrate the supply chain in order to fulfill specific manufacturing goals while respecting expected Key Performance Indicators (KPIs) [5]. Automated planning and scheduling (AI planning) has already proven its potential and could have a huge impact on industrial manufacturing too. It concerns the

---

[3] Cf. https://macropolo.org/digital-projects/supply-chain/ai-chips/ai-chips-supply-chain-mapping.

automated synthesis of autonomous behaviors (i.e., plans) from a model that describes the behavior of the environment in a mathematical and compact form.

Classical planning is one of the most basic models in planning and is concerned with the selection of actions for achieving goals when the initial situation is fully known and actions have deterministic effects [16]. A *classical planning problem* [18] $P = (A, I, \gamma, O)$ consists of a set of state variables A, a description (i.e., a valuation over A) of the initial state of the system I, a goal γ represented as a formula over A, and a list of operations O over A that can lead to state transition. State variables A and actions O constitute the *planning domain* P_D of the planning problem. The solution for a classical planning problem is a sequence of operators (a plan) whose execution transforms the initial state I into a state satisfying the goal G. The computation of the solution may not be an easy task, however, over the years, many algorithms and heuristics have been proposed and embedded into planning systems (known as *planners*) to perform automated planning in an efficient way.

We propose a resilient and scalable approach based on classical planning for the agile orchestration of services aiming at achieving a production goal and adapting to failures by using the framework described in Sect. 2.

The manufacturing resources, represented as services with the Industrial APIs, contain the list of actions runnable by the specific actor modeled in a PDDL-like fashion (PDDL defined in the following). The JSON file describing the services is structured as follows: the *attributes* value is actions-based and each action contains the *parameters*, the *requirements* and the *effects*, both positive and negative, necessary upon the execution of such an action finally, the *features* value contains the characteristics of the actors and their current status.

The *controller* component comprises two sub-modules, i.e., the translator and the planner. The core module of the controller is the *translator*. It transforms the service descriptions (acquired through HTTP requests) and a description of the environmental context (i.e., the production goal and environmental context description) into a planning problem specified in PDDL 2.2. (Planning Domain Definition Language). PDDL [15] is a standard language to describe planning domains and problems. There exist different versions of PDDL which provide an increasing expressive power. The model of the planning problem is separated into two main files: the *domain* and the *problem* descriptions. Such a division allows for an intuitive separation of elements present in every specific problem of the given domain (i.e., types, predicates, functions and actions), and elements that determine the specific problem (i.e., available objects, initial state and goal). The *planner* module represents a planning system able to generate a plan given the domain and problem files. The current prototype of such an approach is based on the FastDownward planner, which supports PDDL 2.2 [20]. The output of the planner, i.e., a plan, contains the list of actions (or operations) needed to reach the final goal by minimizing the total cost.

The *enactor* takes each action contained in the plan file produced by the planner and makes HTTP requests to relative Industrial APIs to perform such actions. Prior to the execution of an action, the current status (a *feature*) of the service is checked. On the one hand, if the status is `available`, the enactor dispatches the action request. On the other hand, if the status is `broken` (meaning that the service is unavailable), the enactor requests the controller the re-calculation of the plan. Particularly, the new plan is generated starting from the current environmental state where one or more services result broken.

4.2 Stochastic Policy

Typically, actors in industrial manufacturing can be thought of as stochastic players. Indeed, their behaviors can be expressed as dependent on a probability that indicates the possibility to act either as functioning or broken actors. In this sense, the manufacturing process becomes a probabilistic planning problem. Adaptivity in such a scenario can be achieved by employing Markov Decision Processes (MDPs) to compose the services representing the manufacturing actors. Particularly, MDPs are able to take into account both the probability and cost of breaking upon the execution of an action enabling a full insight of the entire supply chain.

A MDP [32] is a discrete-time stochastic control process containing *(i)* a set Σ of states which represent the status of the service, *(ii)* a set A of actions i.e., the set of tasks that the service can perform, *(iii)* a transition function P that returns for every state s and action a a distribution over the next state i.e., the probability of the service to end in a certain status performing a certain task, *(iv)* a reward function R that specifies the reward when transitioning from state s to state s' by executing action a, and *(v)* a discount factor $\lambda \in (0,1)$ which determines how important future rewards are to the current state. If $\lambda = 0$, the service is "myopic" in being concerned only with maximizing immediate rewards. As λ approaches 1, the method becomes more "farsighted", more strongly considering future rewards.

By relying on the framework described in Sect. 2, we propose a stochastic policy approach that employs MDPs to orchestrate services in order to produce an adaptive process. A formal description of such an approach is presented in [10].

We define the actors as *stochastic services* modeled as MDPs and maintained by the Industrial APIs. The JSON file describing the characteristic of the actors contains the set of transitions an actor is able to perform and the information relative to the initial, final, and current state. Each actor may represent a *complex breakable service* that includes the set of states (i.e., READY, CONFIGURATION, EXECUTING, BROKEN, REPAIRING) and actions, or may represent a *generic breakable service* that includes a subset of states (i.e., AVAILABLE, DONE, BROKEN) and a subset of actions. Moreover, each actor may represent also *human workers* that can perform the same action of a machine and are preferred when a machine becomes broken, or a *warehouse*. Such an approach allows the flexibility required to model a manufacturing actor operating in its environment. As an example, specific states can be defined to model unavailability conditions (e.g., a broken machine) and the probability of ending in such states. In addition, rewards can be used to model the costs of performing an operation. Different actors can offer the same operation and, as a consequence, an actor chosen for a specific process instance could be discarded for the later instance. The characteristics of the stochastic services is combined into a community of stochastic services, i.e., a *stochastic system service*. Intuitively, the stochastic system service status includes the current status of all the composing services, and a specific action performed on the system service changes only one component of the current state, corresponding to the service selected to execute that action.

Among others, we propose a model to define the manufacturing target by using the concept of *target service*. Such a concept is used to denote a composite service obtained by composing the functions of the stochastic services. Noticeably, the target service itself, as the stochastic services, is a particular case of MDP. However, different from the stochastic services, in the vast majority of cases, the target service is deterministic.

The solution technique of the proposed approach is based on finding an optimal policy for the *composition MDP*. Given the specification of the stochastic system service and the target service, we compute the composition MDP which contains: the cartesian product between all the states of the target service and the stochastic system service, all the actions of the services, the probability of ending in a certain system state performing a system action, and the reward function that is the reward observed from doing a system action summed to the reward coming from the target. In practice, according to a specific target (manufacturing goal), the composition MDP computes all the possible executions of the manufacturing process, i.e., by combining together the specifications of all the actors (stochastic services) and the goal it identifies all the possible status of the actors at any step. The optimal policy of the composition MDP is computed through *policy iteration* and/or *value iteration* [34].

By leveraging on the optimal policy, the *enactor* dispatches the HTTP requests to the chosen services (Industrial APIs) according to the solution. Notice that the policy assigns the services to each action taking into account both probabilities and costs. It is not straightforward indeed to determine a-priori which service a certain action must be assigned to. Additionally, before dispatching the request, it checks whether the current status and the transition functions have changed (for instance because of the wearing out during the execution). We distinguish two different adaptive scenarios. On the one hand, when only the status of an actor changes, the enactor is able to choose the next action to be performed by checking the result of the optimal policy from the new state formed. On the other hand, when both the status and the transition function of an actor change, the enactor requests the re-computation of the optimal policy from an up-to-date composition MDP which includes the latest condition of the service.

4.3 Stochastic Constraint-Based Policy

It is quite common that the manufacturing process is represented using a structured process formalism, such as BPMN or Petri Nets [14]. We are doing more than that, we employ the flexible formalism named DECLARE, directly based on LTL$_f$, to define the manufacturing process. This permits to model the process as a set of logical conditions, so as to more easily specify those processes in which human experience plays a key role or in which the rules of precedence between operations cannot simply be modeled as a sequence.

The proposed technique is an extension of the previous approach. Note that the definitions of both stochastic services and stochastic system service remain the same. By contrast, the target specification of the manufacturing process is represented as an LTL$_f$ formula φ [11] derived from the DECLARE formalization.

The collection of services representing the actors can perform actions in $\mathcal{P}$ and, moreover, to make our model richer we allow services to execute a broader set of actions. In addition, we put each LTL$_f$ formula in conjunction in order to compute the equivalent deterministic finite automaton (DFA) (made by Lydia tool [9]), i.e., *target* DFA.

Given both the stochastic system service and the target DFA we compute the *composition MDP* that in this case contains: the cartesian product between all the states of the target DFA and the stochastic system service, the product between the DFA action and the service that performs the action, the probability of ending in a certain system state performing a system action, and the reward function formed by the reward observed from doing a system action. In practice, according to a specific target (manufacturing goal), the composition MDP computes all the possible executions of the manufacturing process, i.e., by combining together the specifications of all the actors (stochastic services) and the goal (LTL$_f$ formula), it identifies all the possible status of the actors at any step.

We compute the optimal policy of the composition MDP, as in the previous case through *policy iteration* and/or *value iteration* [34]. Such a policy contains the specification of the optimal actions (and related services) to execute from each possible state in order to reach the final goal. The *enactor* acts as a middleware that interfaces with the Industrial APIs in order to check whether the current status and the transition functions have changed (for instance because of the wearing out during the execution). As in the previous approach, we can distinguish two different resilience scenarios. On the one hand, when only the status of an actor changes, the *controller* is able to choose the next action to be performed by checking the result of the optimal policy from the new state formed. On the other hand, when both the status and the transition function of an actor change, the *controller* re-computes the optimal policy from an up-to-date composition MDP which includes the latest condition of the service. Through the Industrial APIs, the *enactor* calls the services identified in the optimal policy computed by the *controller*.

5 Discussing the Approaches

We conduct preliminary tests by applying the proposed approaches to the *Chip-Chain* case study[4].

We divided the case study into two phases, i.e., the collection of the necessary raw materials and chip design and the effective production process. Additionally, we run several experiments by increasing the number of service copies available for the fulfillment of a specific task involved in the process and we measure the execution time and the memory usage. In the following we highlight some important aspects we identify in the results.

Performance values vary greatly depending on the approach used to find the adaptive process. In the planning approach, increasing the number of services, time and memory consumption does not change significantly. This is possible because planning solvers employ well-known heuristics able to derive, in an efficient way, a solution. However, this approach does not consider the stochasticity typical of an industrial context. In particular, does not take into account for example the probability for a certain machine to end in a failure situation, represented instead in the stochastic approaches.

On the other hand, the values of the stochastic policy approaches increase exponentially, as the number of services increases. This happens because of the definition of the composition MDP. It consists of a cartesian product operation that takes into account both the target and system service sets. Although the target is static and well-defined, the system service may increase with the added services resulting in an increment of memory consumption and execution time. Additionally, the stochastic constraint-based policy approach is more time and memory consuming with respect to the stochastic policy approach. This notable difference derives from the target service concept where we define a set of logical constraints between actions. Also, we consider the "auxiliary actions", i.e., actions that do not concern the process being realized but are needed by the services to get ready for the execution of main actions.

Even though planning is often a more effective strategy, it may not be the only factor to consider when it comes to production. Depending on the situation, it is necessary to take into account not just how quickly calculations are performed but also how the system is modeled and responds to unknown events. As they reflect the stochasticity behaviors in the manufacturing domains, both the stochastic techniques, which end up being much slower than planning, offer more expressive power.

The proposed approaches are based on the definition of constraints regarding the process execution. Depending on the used approach, such constraints are modeled in a different way. The approach based on planning requires not to be generic in the specification of the actions which are essential in the computation

---

[4] Source codes of the implemented approaches, and tests, are available for repeatability the instance planning approach at https://tinyurl.com/instanceplanning and the two stochastic policy approaches at https://tinyurl.com/stochasticpolicy. The source code of the Industrial APIs layer is available at https://tinyurl.com/IndustrialAPIs.

of the plan (given a goal). On the other hand, it permits to model the involved objects by monitoring the production progress.

The approach based on stochastic policy requires a full definition of the manufacturing process (defined as an automaton). This is different in its extension which employs LTL$_f$. Here the process is defined by specifying constraints between the tasks. In the modeling, we do not include relationship effects possibly existing between the services (e.g., if the service A is used, then service B cannot be used). In the case of planning, this type of constraint could be modeled with the PDDL conditional effects which, however, have consequences in the computation costs. It is not easy to model this behavior in the stochastic policy approaches because the target service only knows manufacturing tasks and has no idea of the services employed. A possibility could be to introduce related constraints when the composition MDP is computed. Anyway, in this paper, we model such constraints by increasing the services costs of affected services.

Moreover, in this paper we focus on a case study focusing on a batch production, i.e., production of a batch of one product [19]. In this sense, we study the adaptivity by taking into consideration the fact that a specific task of the supply chain production is executed on a batch, thus if a decision is taken at the beginning of a task, it is maintained until the end of it. Such an approach influences adaptivity by discarding the possibility of adapting the production inside a specific batch and considering only the adaptivity at the end of a task.

6   Related Works

In this paper, we focus on approaches leveraging automated reasoning techniques to enable adaptation in smart manufacturing, specifically in the supply chain context. We can contextualize our work in the broader research area that applies automated planning techniques. We refer to automated planning as the application of AI technologies to the problem of generating a correct and efficient sequence of actions [28]. Furthermore, we can distinguish between classical planning, which deals with deterministic scenarios, and so-called decision-theoretic planning [4], which deals with stochastic behavior.

Examples of classical planning in smart manufacturing are provided in several works. The authors in [29] employ automated planning in order to cope with exceptional and unanticipated events. In particular, planning is employed to fix a process instance, restoring the conditions to continue with the standard, manually defined process. In [35], the authors show how to plan the assembly of small trucks from available components and how to assign specific production operations to available production resources. In [27], the authors develop an evaluation with a physical smart factory that resolves detected exceptional situations and continues process execution. However, all the solutions based on classical planning do not consider a crucial aspect of manufacturing production, i.e., the uncertainty typical of the entire production process and of the manufacturing actors.

The application of decision-theoretic planning approaches might be a solution. An example is [8], where the authors define a set of degrading planning domains.

The planner tries to find a solution in the most restrictive, optimal domain. If during the execution, assumptions of a plan are not verified, due for example to failures, more and more sub-optimal domains are employed. The approach focuses on the entire process and the non-determinism of manufacturing actors is modeled. Furthermore, MDPs are a widely used model for decision-making problems.

Nevertheless, the literature presents limited research on the application of MDPs in the manufacturing domain. Authors in [21] propose a self-adaptive Automated Guided Vehicles (AGVs) control model, depicted as an MDP, that enables AGVs to avoid collisions efficiently, safely, and economically. The work [7] presents a hierarchical MDP approach for adaptive multi-scale prognostics and health management for smart manufacturing systems. The goal is to create a policy for making sequential decisions that will maximize the expected gain under the set of constraints. Authors in [2] use an MDP for finding an optimal cost-effective maintenance decision based on the condition revealed at the time of inspection on a single diesel engine. In these cases, the use of MDPs fits very well in the manufacturing context and in particular non-deterministic domains, because it always allows making the best choice.

Finally, in this paper, we discuss how to solve triple-A and resilience in smart manufacturing processes by adopting a service-based approach and automated reasoning techniques; this is not completely new, at least in the service computing literature, as seminal approaches go to [24] and more recently to [23]. An interesting survey on how planning techniques, not including MDPs, have been applied to service composition problems is [17].

7   Concluding Remarks

In this paper, we have proposed and discussed how automated reasoning techniques can be employed with the goal of adaptivity and resilience in smart manufacturing supply chains. The need for these techniques emerges when the number of resources involved and the constraints among them make a manual analysis from human experts unfeasible. In this sense, we have outlined and discussed the application of several techniques to a challenging use case concerning the manufacturing of integrated circuits. Our service-based approach, and its application to smart manufacturing, is another example of the challenges that service composition will have to cope in the next few years, as discussed in [1].

With respect to AI, in this paper, we only consider automated reasoning, without showing the potential of applying machine learning (especially reinforcement learning) techniques. If, on the one hand, machine learning approaches do not require any manual modeling effort, they usually require datasets to be trained, which are difficult to obtain in the smart manufacturing scenario, especially at a supply chain scale.

Also, this paper does not include approaches from classical numerical optimization techniques. These techniques are available in the form of very fast implementations. The main drawback is that modeling must be done in the form of equations, which are more complex to compose and validate with respect to formalisms employed in automated reasoning.

Acknowledgements. This work is partially funded by the ERC project WhiteMech (no. 834228), the PRIN project RIPER (no. 20203FFYLK), the Electrospindle 4.0 project (funded by Ministero per lo Sviluppo Economico, Italy, no. F/160038/01-04/X41), the Piano Nazionale di Ripresa e Resilienza (PNRR), Missione 4 "Istruzione e ricerca" - Componente 2 "Dalla ricerca all'impresa" - Investimento 1.3, funded by European Union - NextGenerationEU, and in particular by PE1 (CUP B53C22003980006) and PE11 (CUP B53C22004130001).

References

1. Aiello, M.: A challenge for the next 50 years of automated service composition. In: Troya, J., Medjahed, B., Piattini, M., Yao, L., Fernández, P., Ruiz-Cortés, A. (eds.) Service-Oriented Computing - 20th International Conference, ICSOC 2022, Proceedings. LNCS, vol. 13740, pp. 635–643. Springer, Cham (2022). https://doi.org/10.1007/978-3-031-20984-0_45
2. Amari, S.V., McLaughlin, L., Pham, H.: Cost-effective condition-based maintenance using Markov decision processes. In: RAMS 2006. Annual Reliability and Maintainability Symposium, pp. 464–469. IEEE (2006)
3. Bicocchi, N., Cabri, G., Mandreoli, F., Mecella, M.: Dynamic digital factories for agile supply chains: an architectural approach. J. Ind. Inf. Integr. **15**, 111–121 (2019)
4. Blythe, J.: Decision-theoretic planning. AI Mag. **20**(2), 37 (1999)
5. Catarci, T., Firmani, D., Leotta, F., Mandreoli, F., Mecella, M., Sapio, F.: A conceptual architecture and model for smart manufacturing relying on service-based digital twins. In: 2019 IEEE International Conference on Web Services (ICWS), pp. 229–236. IEEE (2019)
6. Chen, H.Y., Das, A., Ivanov, D.: Building resilience and managing post-disruption supply chain recovery: lessons from the information and communication technology industry. Int. J. Inf. Manage. **49**, 330–342 (2019)
7. Choo, B.Y., Adams, S.C., Weiss, B.A., Marvel, J.A., Beling, P.A.: Adaptive multiscale prognostics and health management for smart manufacturing systems. Int. J. Prognostics Health Manage. **7**, 014 (2016)
8. Ciolek, D., D'Ippolito, N., Pozanco, A., Sardiña, S.: Multi-tier automated planning for adaptive behavior. In: Proceedings of the International Conference on Automated Planning and Scheduling, vol. 30, pp. 66–74 (2020)
9. De Giacomo, G., Favorito, M.: Compositional approach to translate LTLF/LDLF into deterministic finite automata. In: ICAPS, pp. 122–130. AAAI Press (2021)
10. De Giacomo, G., Favorito, M., Leotta, F., Mecella, M., Silo, L.: Digital twins composition in smart manufacturing via Markov decision processes. Comput. Ind. **149**, 103916 (2023)
11. De Giacomo, G., Vardi, M.Y.: Linear temporal logic and linear dynamic logic on finite traces. In: IJCAI 2013 Proceedings of the Twenty-Third International Joint Conference on Artificial Intelligence, pp. 854–860 (2013)
12. Dubey, R., Gunasekaran, A., Childe, S.J.: The design of a responsive sustainable supply chain network under uncertainty. Int. J. Adv. Manuf. Technol. **80**, 427–445 (2015)
13. Dumas, M., et al.: Ai-augmented business process management systems: a research manifesto. ACM Trans. Manage. Inf. Syst. **14**(1), 1–19 (2023)

14. Dumas, M., La Rosa, M., Mendling, J., Reijers, H.A.: Fundamentals of Business Process Management. Springer, Heidelberg (2013). https://doi.org/10.1007/978-3-662-56509-4

15. Fox, M., Long, D.: PDDL2.1: an extension to PDDL for expressing temporal planning domains. J. Artif. Intell. Res. **20**, 61–124 (2003)

16. Geffner, H.: Computational models of planning. Wiley Interdisc. Rev. Cogn. Sci. **4**(4), 341–356 (2013)

17. Georgievski, I., Aiello, M.: Automated planning for ubiquitous computing. ACM Comput. Surv. **49**(4), 63:1–63:46 (2017)

18. Ghallab, M., Nau, D., Traverso, P.: Automated Planning and Acting. Cambridge University Press, Cambridge (2016)

19. Groover, M.P.: Automation, Production Systems, and Computer-Integrated Manufacturing. Pearson Education India (2016)

20. Helmert, M.: The fast downward planning system. J. Artif. Intell. Res. **26**, 191–246 (2006)

21. Hu, H., Jia, X., Liu, K., Sun, B.: Self-adaptive traffic control model with behavior trees and reinforcement learning for AGV in Industry 4.0. IEEE Trans. Ind. Inform. **17**(12), 7968–7979 (2021)

22. Ivanov, D., Dolgui, A., Sokolov, B., Ivanova, M.: Literature review on disruption recovery in the supply chain. Int. J. Prod. Res. **55**(20), 6158–6174 (2017)

23. Kaldeli, E., Lazovik, A., Aiello, M.: Domain-independent planning for services in uncertain and dynamic environments. Artif. Intell. **236**, 30–64 (2016)

24. Lazovik, A., Aiello, M., Papazoglou, M.: Planning and monitoring the execution of web service requests. In: Orlowska, M.E., Weerawarana, S., Papazoglou, M.P., Yang, J. (eds.) ICSOC 2003. LNCS, vol. 2910, pp. 335–350. Springer, Heidelberg (2003). https://doi.org/10.1007/978-3-540-24593-3_23

25. Lee, H.L., et al.: The triple-A supply chain. Harvard Bus. Rev. **82**(10), 102–113 (2004)

26. Macher, J.T., Mowery, D.C., Simcoe, T.S.: e-business and disintegration of the semiconductor industry value chain. Ind. Innov. **9**(3), 155–181 (2002)

27. Malburg, L., Hoffmann, M., Bergmann, R.: Applying MAPE-K control loops for adaptive workflow management in smart factories. J. Intell. Inf. Syst. **61**, 83–111 (2023)

28. Marrella, A.: Automated planning for business process management. J. Data Semant. **8**(2), 79–98 (2019)

29. Marrella, A., Mecella, M., Sardina, S.: Intelligent process adaptation in the SmartPM system. ACM Trans. Intell. Syst. Technol. **8**(2), 1–43 (2016)

30. Marrella, A., Mecella, M., Sardiña, S.: Supporting adaptiveness of cyber-physical processes through action-based formalisms. AI Commun. **31**(1), 47–74 (2018)

31. Paul, S.K., Chowdhury, P.: Strategies for managing the impacts of disruptions during COVID-19: an example of toilet paper. Global J. Flexible Syst. Manage **21**, 283–293 (2020)

32. Puterman, M.L.: Markov Decision Processes (1994)

33. Stadtler, H.: Supply chain management: an overview. In: Stadtler, H., Kilger, C. (eds.) Supply Chain Management and Advanced Planning: Concepts, Models, Software, and Case Studies, pp. 3–28. Springer, Heidelberg (2015). https://doi.org/10.1007/978-3-540-74512-9_2

34. Sutton, R.S., Barto, A.G.: Reinforcement Learning: An Introduction (2018)

35. Wally, B., et al.: Leveraging iterative plan refinement for reactive smart manufacturing systems. IEEE Trans. Autom. Sci. Eng. **18**(1), 230–243 (2020)

Pool Games in Various Information Environments

Constantinos Varsos[1]([envelope])[iD] and Marina Bitsaki[2][iD]

[1] Centrum Wiskunde & Informatica, Amsterdam 1098 XG, The Netherlands
Konstantinos.Varsos@cwi.nl
[2] University of Crete, Heraklion 700 13 Crete, Greece
marina@csd.uoc.gr

Abstract. The emergence of Blockchain digital technology provides one of the most prominent transaction mechanisms in an increasing variety of digital and augmented environments. In the Blockchain habitat, interactions among autonomous agents, called miners, form mining pools that aggregate computational power in order to increase their possible gains. A Pool game models mining pools that compete against each other in order to improve their outcome by strategically committing their miners. Current studies in Pool games make the assumption that pools have complete and correct information about the situation. In this work we drop this assumption, studying Pool games under various information environments such as incomplete information and erroneous information.

Keywords: Pool games · misinformation games · Bayesian games

1 Introduction

Nowadays, the emergence of digital environments, automated procedures, and big data have brought into light many intangible, crowd-sourcing, and sophisticated digital transaction methodologies. One of the emerging attractive solutions that provide security, accessibility, and privacy in big data systems is the Blockchain, see [3]. It was proposed in [12] to serve as the main concept in the digital economy, providing transparent and secure transactions in distributed and decentralized environments (for more details see [5]). Hence, Blockchain technology provides an appealing and applicable methodology for versatile practices from Insurance and Commerce to the Internet of Things and Security.

In practice, a Blockchain is a distributed synchronized secure database containing validated blocks of transactions. A block is validated by special nodes, called miners, via the solution of a computationally demanding problem, called the proof-of-work puzzle. The miners compete against each other and the first one to solve the problem, provides a full proof of work, and announces it. The block is then verified by a predefined agreement protocol called consensus. After

Supported by ERCIM.

the new block reaches the consensus, it is added to the distributed database, and the miner that generated the block is rewarded according to the, commonly and a priori known, protocol of the transaction.

In order to increase their outcome, miners form mining pools implemented by a pool manager (see [10]), where all of them provide proof of work concurrently and share their revenues accordingly. In this work, we focus on open pools that allow any miner to join them. The utility of a pool is the total sum of the revenues received by its miners. The information available to a pool includes the set of its miners, a predefined protocol for the reward of newly generated blocks, and the set of adversary pools.

As stated in [4], a miner may attack an adversary pool by providing partial proof of work to its pool manager. The attacking miner shares the revenue obtained in the pool but does not contribute, thus the utility of the attacked pool deteriorates and becomes less attractive to other miners.

Therefore, pools may have incentives to commit miners attack and deliver partial proof of work (called infiltration rate) to opponent pools in order to improve their revenues, see [10]. Hence, the use of game-theoretical tools in the Blockchain environment is a direct way to study, model and analyze these kinds of interactions (see [1,4,11]).

In the literature, pools are aware of the number of miners at their disposal and can estimate accurately the amount of attacking miners. Thus, they have complete and correct information regarding the interaction with other pools. This is a highly unrealistic scenario, as, in many situations, none of these assumptions hold, due to the presence of side information, bounded rationality, computational restrictions, etc. In this paper, we study the Pool game considering various information environments as stated in the following subsection.

1.1   Contributions

A pool manager may experience several scenarios for modeling uncertainty or erroneous beliefs with regards to the mining power (how many miners) or the infiltration rate (how many attackers) of a pool. In order to cope with these issues and provide a more realistic analysis of the Pool game setting, we plug in the model of [4] incomplete and incorrect information, considering two cases.

First, we address the case where the pools have incomplete information regarding the infiltration situation. In particular, the pools are not aware of the size of the incoming attack. In Subsect. 4.1, we model this scenario using the notion of Bayesian games as provided in [9], prove the convergence of revenues and compute the equilibria of the Bayesian Pool game.

Second, in Subsect. 4.2, we consider the case where the pools have incorrect information regarding the specifications of the interaction. More specifically, they think they know the actual mining power of the pool and the accurate number of incoming attacks. We model this scenario using the concept of misinformation games as introduced in [16]. In order to cope with the iterative nature of the Pool game, we apply the *Adaptation Procedure*, which was introduced in [14]. Hence, the misinformed pools have the machinery to re-evaluate their information and adapt their decisions in the next round. We prove the convergence of the revenues and compute the equilibria of the misinformed Pool game.

Another contribution of this work is about the convergence of the revenues of the Pool games for the case of complete-correct information. Namely, in Lemma 1, Theorem 1, and Corollary 1 we prove the convergence of the density revenues for non-constant infiltration rates, as opposed to Lemma 1 in [4].

Summarizing the various information scenarios, in the correct-complete case, [4], the pools know their mining power and estimate correctly the infiltration rates. In the setting of incomplete information, pools know their mining power but assign probabilities in the infiltration rate. In the setting of incorrect information, pools know incorrectly their mining power and the infiltration rates they face. Throughout our analysis, we assume that all of the pools are of equal capabilities and all miners are identical.

2   Related Work

Several studies cope with complete and correct information settings (e.g. [2,4]). The Pool game is presented in detail in [4]. A different approach is introduced in [2], where the authors provide allocation methodologies so that the miners cooperate, and avoid the development of centralized pools. In the same spirit, in [8,17] authors introduced models where the miners can either cooperate or employ a block withholding attack in a pool. In [10] authors study the Pool game model, in the complete-correct information environment, from the perspective of system rewards and punishments and analyze the outcome of the interaction. Further, in [7] authors study models, where miners play a complete-information stochastic game from the perspective of miners. In this study, we focus on the cases of incomplete and incorrect information.

In the context of Bayesian games, authors in [19] consider the case where a user knows the distribution of others' valuations, and focuses on truthful mechanisms. In [18] authors propose a characterization of Blockchain protocols regarding the rational and Byzantine behaviors. Furthermore, in [6] authors present a probabilistic model based on the information propagating over a Blockchain habitat (e.g. a Bitcoin network). They probabilistically identify the users initiating the transactions and do not implement their framework in the case of incomplete information. Authors in [15] plug in Bayesian game theory into Blockchain transactions, and provide an auction model.

In summary, existing works that apply game theory in Blockchain environments with incomplete information, mainly focus on the development of sufficient and robust mechanisms that regulate the situation, rather than on interactions among pools. To the best of our knowledge, there are no works that deal with the situation where pools experience subjective views of information.

3   Preliminaries

We consider a normal-form *game* $G = \langle N, S, U \rangle$ that consists of a set of players N, a set $S = S_1 \times \ldots \times S_{|N|}$ of players' joint decisions, where S_i is player's

i set of pure strategies and a utility matrix $U = (U_1, \ldots, U_{|N|})$, where $U_i \in \mathbb{R}^{|S_1| \times \cdots \times |S_{|N|}|}$ is player's i utility matrix.

A mixed strategy for player i that represents a probabilistic mixture of pure strategies, is a tuple $\sigma_i = (\sigma_{i1}, \ldots, \sigma_{i|S_i|})$ where $\sigma_{ij} \geq 0$ and $\sum_j \sigma_{ij} = 1$. Let Σ_i be the set of all possible mixed strategies of player i. In a game with $|N|$ players, a strategy profile is an $|N|$-tuple $\sigma = (\sigma_1, \ldots, \sigma_{|N|})$, $\sigma_i \in \Sigma_i$, and σ_{-i} is the strategy profile all but player i. Further, we will use the Forbenius norm $\| \cdot \| : \mathbb{R}^{n \times m} \to \mathbb{R}$ in Sect. 4.

The players' behaviour in a normal-form game is predicted through the *Nash equilibrium*:

Definition 1 (Nash equilibrium [13]). *A strategy profile $\sigma^* = (\sigma_1^*, \ldots, \sigma_{|N|}^*)$ is a Nash equilibrium, if and only if, for any i and for any $\sigma_i \in \Sigma_i$, $f_i(\sigma_i^*, \sigma_{-i}^*) \geq f_i(\sigma_i, \sigma_{-i}^*)$, where f_i is the utility function of player i, defined as $f_i : \Sigma \to \mathbb{R}$, such that:*

$$f_i(\sigma_i, \sigma_{-i}) = \sum_{k \in S_1} \cdots \sum_{j \in S_{|N|}} U_i(k, \ldots, j) \cdot \sigma_{1,k} \cdot \ldots \cdot \sigma_{|N|,j}, \tag{1}$$

We denote a Nash equilibrium by ne and the set of nes in G by $NE(G)$.

3.1 Incomplete Information

In classical game theory, incomplete information is addressed by Bayesian games. A Bayesian normal-form game is defined as a tuple $BG = \langle N, S, \Theta, p, U \rangle$, where N, S are defined as previously. $\Theta = \Theta_1 \times \ldots \times \Theta_{|N|}$ is the set of joint types of players, p is a common prior distribution over the types, and U is the set of utility functions, $U = (U_1, \ldots, U_N)$, whereas $U_i : (S \times \Theta)_i \to \mathbb{R}$.

A player's type is private information and is used to make decisions and update her beliefs about the likelihood of opponents' types (using the conditional probability $p(\theta_{-i}|\theta_i)$, where $\theta_i \in \Theta_i$). In this setting, a pure strategy is given by a mapping from the type space to the strategy space, $s_i : \Theta_i \to S_i$. In other words, s_i maps every information type $\theta_i \in \Theta_i$ that player i has to the pure strategy that she could play in that type. As in the case of correct-complete information, a mixed strategy σ_i is a probabilistic mixture of pure strategies.

Each player calculates her expected utility given that she knows her own type but not the types of the opponents (*ex-interim* concept)[1] by the following formula,

$$\mathbb{E}[U_i(\sigma, \theta_i)] = \sum_{\theta_{-i} \in \Theta_{-i}} p(\theta_{-i}|\theta_i) \mathbb{E}[U_i(\sigma, (\theta_i, \theta_{-i}))], \tag{2}$$

where θ_i is the type of player i.

Player i's best response curve to strategy profile σ_{-i} is given by $BR_i(\sigma_{-i}) = \arg\max_{\sigma_i \in \Sigma_i} \mathbb{E}[U(\sigma_i, \sigma_{-i})]$.

Definition 2 (Bayes-Nash equilibrium, [9]). *A Bayes-Nash equilibrium is a mixed-strategy profile σ such that $\sigma_i \in BR_i(\sigma_{-i}), \forall i \in N$.*

---

[1] There are also the concepts of *ex-post*, and *ex-ante* utilities, see [9].

Repeated Bayesian Games Consider a finite discrete time horizon T, with $T > 0$. In our study we will analyze two cases: i) undiscounted utilities, and ii) discounted utilities. In the first case, the utilities in BG are evaluated as limits of arithmetic averages. In the latter case, we allow every player to evaluate her utility sequence with a discount factor $\delta \in (0, 1)$. The utility formulas for both cases are provided by Table 1. Further, the players' types are intrinsic characteristics and are fixed throughout the interaction.

Table 1. Utility formulas for the repeated Bayesian game.

case	formula	
Undiscounted	$\frac{1}{T} \sum_{t \in [T]} U_i(\sigma^t, \theta_i)$	$i \in [|N|], T > 0$
Discounted	$(1 - \delta) \sum_{t \in [T]} \delta^t U_i(\sigma^t, \theta_i)$	

3.2   Incorrect Information

Misinformation games were introduced in [16] and defined as a tuple $mG = \langle G^0, G^1, \ldots, G^{|N|} \rangle$, where all G^i are normal-form games and G^0 contains $|N|$ players. Further, G^0 is called the *actual game* and represents the game that is actually being played, whereas G^i $(i \in N)$ represents the game that player i thinks that is being played (called the *game of player i*). Moreover, no assumptions are made as to the relation among G^0 and G^is, thereby allowing all types of misinformation.

The outcome of a misinformation game is dictated by the equilibrium strategy profiles that each player picks in her view.

Definition 3 (Natural misinformed equilibrium). *A strategy profile* $\sigma^* = (\sigma_1^{*,1}, \ldots, \sigma_{|N|}^{*,|N|})$ *is a natural misinformed equilibrium, if and only if, for any i and for any $\hat{\sigma}_i \in \Sigma_i^i$, $f_i^i(\sigma^{*,i}, \sigma_{-i}^{*,i}) \geq f_i^i(\hat{\sigma}_i, \sigma_{-i}^{*,i})$, where f^i is the utility function of player i in the game G^i and defined as: $f_i^i : \Sigma^i \to \mathbb{R}$, such that:*

$$f_i^i(\sigma_i^i, \sigma_{-i}^i) = \sum_{k \in S_1^i} \cdots \sum_{j \in S_{|N|}^i} U_i^i(k, \ldots, j) \cdot \sigma_{1,k}^i \cdot \ldots \cdot \sigma_{|N|,j}^i, \quad (3)$$

Further, we denote by $NME(mG)$ the set of *nmes* in mG. Observe that players obtain the utilities provided by G^0, and not the utilities they realise in G^is.

Evidently, the misinformed players may come across an outcome different than the one they expect in their own game. In the case where the interaction is iterative, the misinformed players update their information according to choices they made, the choices their opponents have made, and the corresponding information that the environment provides to them. This process is formalized by the *Adaptation Procedure* that was introduced in [14]. More specifically, the Adaptation Procedure occurs in discrete time steps $t \in \mathbb{N}_0 = \mathbb{N} \cup \{0\}$. It starts at $t = 0$ with the misinformation game mG. Then, at each time step $t \geq 0$, the players choose a Nash strategy profile in their game, and new *nmes* are formed. As the outcome and the respective utilities are announced, the players re-adjust their choices and update their utilities according to the information they have received. Formally, the Adaptation Procedure is provided by the following definition.

Definition 4 (Definition 4.4 in [14]). *For a set M of misinformation games, we set $\mathcal{AD}(M) = \{mG_u \mid mG \in M, u \in \chi(\sigma), \sigma \in NME(mG)\}$. We define as Adaptation Procedure of a set of misinformation games M to be the iterative process such that:*

$$\begin{cases} \mathcal{AD}^{(0)}(M) = M \\ \mathcal{AD}^{(t+1)}(M) = \mathcal{AD}^{(t)}(\mathcal{AD}(M)) \end{cases}$$

for $t \in \mathbb{N}_0$.

where $\chi(\sigma)$ is the set of indices associated with the strategies in the support of the strategy profile σ and mG_u is the updated game. Namely, u provides the position in the subjective utility matrices where the update takes place, and is determined by the strategic choices of the players.

The Adaptation Procedure terminates (see Definition 4.5 in [14]), if there exists a time point $t \in \mathbb{N}_0$ such that any further iterations do not provide new information to the players, that is $\mathcal{AD}^{(t+1)}(M) = \mathcal{AD}^{(t)}(M)$. Interestingly, the *nme* where the players do not obtain new information is stable; this is called stable misinformed equilibrium *sme*. We denote by $SME(mG)$ the set of *smes* in mG.

4   The Pool Game

We consider the case where a set of N pools, with a total of m miners, compete with each other in order to maximize their outcome. This situation is introduced in [4] as the Pool game. In particular, the pools try to maximize their revenue density by optimizing their infiltration rates to the adversaries. As stated in [4], the revenue density of pool i is the ratio between the average revenue that miner v earns and the average revenue it would have earned as a solo miner. We denote the revenue density of pool i at time step t by $r_i(t)$.

In this study, the interaction is evolved in discrete time steps, and the total number of miners that each pool has in its disposal remains constant throughout the game. Moreover, each pool can compare the rates of partial and full proofs of work it receives from its miners, in order to find the rate of infiltrators attacking it, see [4]. Also, it can compute the revenue rates of each of the other pools. Initially, we restate the basic concepts of Pool games in the case where each pool has correct and complete information about the infiltration rates and the density revenue.

Let $m_i(t)$ be the total number of miners in the disposal of pool i, whereas $m_{ii}(t)$ is the number of miners pool i assigns to mine honestly in pool i, and

$m_{ij}(t)$ is the number of miners used by pool i to infiltrate pool j at time step t (infiltration rate). Thus, in general, it holds $m_i(t) \geq \sum_j m_{ij}(t)$. Clearly, in each time step pool i mines with power $m_{ii}(t)$, and shares its reward among $m_i(t) + \sum_{j \in [|N|] \setminus \{i\}} m_{ji}(t)$ members. For our analysis we use the following vector that measures the direct mining revenue density,

$$\mathbf{u}(t) = \left(\frac{m_1(t) - \sum_{j \in [|N|] \setminus \{1\}} m_{1j}(t)}{m_1(t) + \sum_{j \in [|N|] \setminus \{1\}} m_{j1}(t)}, \ldots, \frac{m_N(t) - \sum_{j \in [|N|] \setminus \{N\}} m_{Nj}(t)}{m_N(t) + \sum_{j \in [|N|] \setminus \{N\}} m_{jN}(t)} \right)^T$$

Further, in time step t pool i gains revenue $m_{ij}(t) r_j(t-1)$ through infiltrating pool j with $m_{ij}(t)$ miners, and distributes it among members $m_i(t) + \sum_{j \in [|N|]} m_{ji}(t)$. We construct the $|N| \times |N|$ infiltration matrix as follows

$$\mathbf{IR}(t) = \begin{pmatrix} \frac{m_{11}(t)}{m_1(t) + \sum_j m_{j1}(t)} & \cdots & \frac{m_{1|N|}(t)}{m_1(t) + \sum_j m_{j1}(t)} \\ \vdots & \ddots & \vdots \\ \frac{m_{|N|1}(t)}{m_{|N|}(t) + \sum_j m_{j|N|}(t)} & \cdots & \frac{m_{|N||N|}(t)}{m_{|N|}(t) + \sum_j m_{j|N|}(t)} \end{pmatrix} \tag{4}$$

Plugin together the $\mathbf{u}(t)$ and $\mathbf{IR}(t)$ we end up with the density revenue vector at time step t,

$$\mathbf{r}(t) = \mathbf{u}(t) + \mathbf{IR}(t) \cdot \mathbf{r}(t-1) \text{ with } \mathbf{r}(0) = \mathbf{u}(0) \tag{5}$$

Moreover, the direct mining rate, $R_i(t)$, of pool i at time step t, is the number of its miners, $m_i(t)$, minus the miners it uses for infiltration, $\sum_{j \in [|N|] \setminus \{i\}} m_{ij}(t)$, and is divided by the total mining rate in the system, namely the number of all miners apart from the perpetrators. So, we have the following formula

$$R_i(t) = \frac{m_i(t) - \sum_{j \in [|N|] \setminus \{i\}} m_{ij}(t)}{m - \sum_{j \in [|N|] \setminus \{i\}} \sum_{k \in [|N|] \setminus \{j\}} m_{jk}(t)} \tag{6}$$

Hence, for the revenue density of pool i we have

$$r_i(t) = \frac{R_i(t) + \sum_{j \in [|N|] \setminus \{i\}} m_{ij}(t) r_j(t)}{m_i(t) + \sum_{j \in [|N|] \setminus \{i\}} m_{ji}(t)} \tag{7}$$

with that we define the revenue density vector $\mathbf{r}(t) = (r_1(t), \ldots, r_n(t))^T$. In case where $|n| = 2$, the infiltration rates are $m_{12}(t)$ and $m_{21}(t)$, and the formula (7) takes the form

$$r_1(m_{12}(t), m_{21}(t)) = \frac{m_{22}(t) R_1(t) + m_{12}(t)(R_1(t) + R_2(t))}{m_{11}(t) m_{22}(t) + m_{11}(t) m_{12}(t) + m_{22}(t) m_{21}(t)},$$

$$r_2(m_{12}(t), m_{21}(t)) = \frac{m_{11}(t) R_2(t) + m_{21}(t)(R_1(t) + R_2(t))}{m_{11}(t) m_{22}(t) + m_{11}(t) m_{12}(t) + m_{22}(t) m_{21}(t)} \tag{8}$$

with $m_{11}(t), m_{22}(t) > 0$ and $m_1(t) + m_2(t) \leq m$. Further, each pool controls only its own infiltration rate. In each round of the Pool game, each pool will optimize its infiltration rate of the other. Clearly, an equilibrium exists where neither Pool$_1$ nor Pool$_2$ can improve its revenue by changing its infiltration rate.

As stated in [4], the values of $m_{12}(t), m_{21}(t)$ at the equilibrium can be computed by solving the following system of first-order ordinary differential equations

$$\begin{cases} \dfrac{\partial r_1(m_{12}(t), m_{21}(t))}{\partial m_{12}(t)} = 0 \\ \dfrac{\partial r_2(m_{12}(t), m_{21}(t))}{\partial m_{21}(t)} = 0 \end{cases} \tag{9}$$

In the rest of the analysis we assume that pool i has two pure strategies; attack or to non-attack the adversary. The density revenue for the pure strategy attack is r_i, and for the pure strategy non-attack is $\tilde{r}_i$. Hence the pure strategy profiles are (attack, attack), (attack, non-attack), (non-attack, attack), and (non-attack, non-attack). Moreover, from [4] we have the following ordering for the density revenues of the pools

$$\text{For Pool}_1 : \begin{cases} (attack, non - attack) > (non - attack, non - attack) \\ (attack, attack) > (non - attack, attack) \end{cases}$$

$$\text{For Pool}_2 : \begin{cases} (non - attack, attack) > (non - attack, non - attack) \\ (attack, attack) > (attack, non - attack) \end{cases} \tag{10}$$

With this at hand we can produce the payoff matrix as provided in Table 2.

Table 2. Pool game with two pools, Fig. 9 in [4].

Pool$_2$ / Pool$_1$	attack	non-attack
attack	(r_1, r_2)	$(r_1, \tilde{r}_2)$
non-attack	$(\tilde{r}_1, r_2)$	$(\tilde{r}_1, \tilde{r}_2)$

Observe that the game provided by Table 2 is a Prisoner's Dilemma, meaning that $(attack, attack)$ is a dominating pure strategy profile.

Moreover, in [4] it is proved that the pool revenues converge, in the case where infiltration rates are constant. In the following we prove that the convergence of density revenues holds for cases where the infiltration rates are not constant.

Lemma 1. *Consider a Pool game with $|N|$ pools, and $m_i(t)$, $m_{ij}(t)$ non-zero polynomials of equal degree $d \in \mathbb{N}$ with non-negative coefficients $\forall i, j \in [|N|]$ and $\forall t \in \mathbb{N}$. Then the pool density revenues converge.*

Proof. Let $m_i(t) = \sum_{k\in[d]} \alpha_{i,k} t^k$ and $m_{ij}(t) = \sum_{k\in[d]} \beta_{ij,k} t^k$, with $\alpha_{i,k}, \beta_{ij,k} \geq 0$ $\forall i, j, k$. Observe that the elements of the $\mathbf{IR}(t)$ are

$$(\mathbf{IR}(t))_{ij} = \frac{m_{ii}(t)}{m_i(t) + \sum_j m_{ji}(t)} = \frac{\sum_{k\in[d]} \beta_{ii,k} t^k}{\sum_{k\in[d]} \alpha_{i,k} t^k + \sum_j \sum_{k\in[d]} \beta_{ji,k} t^k}$$

Hence taking the limit we have,

$$\lim_{t\to+\infty} (\mathbf{IR}(t))_{ij} = \lim_{t\to+\infty} \frac{\sum_{k\in[d]} \beta_{ii,k} t^{k-d}}{\sum_{k\in[d]} \alpha_{i,k} t^{k-d} + \sum_j \sum_{k\in[d]} \beta_{ji,k} t^{k-d}} = \frac{\beta_{ii,d}}{\alpha_{i,d} + \sum_j \beta_{ji,d}}$$

In the $(\mathbf{IR}(t))_{ij}$ the denominator can not be equal to 0, as $m_i(t)$, $m_{ij}(t)$ are non-zero polynomials. Hence, on the limit the $\mathbf{IR}(t)$ has constant elements, then using Lemma 1 in [4] we conclude. □

In the rest of the analysis, we consider $\mathbf{m}_i(t)$ as non-negative and continuous functions in time $\forall i$, and we have the following result

Theorem 1. *Consider a Pool game with $|N|$ pools, with bounded $\mathbf{u}(t)$, and $\mathbf{IR}(t)$ such that $\|\mathbf{IR}(t)\| \leq 1 \, \forall t \in \mathbf{N}$. Then the pool density revenues converges to $\mathbf{u}(t)$.*

Proof. From the Eq. (5) we have

$$\mathbf{r}(t) - \mathbf{u}(t) = \sum_{k=1}^{t} \left(\prod_{d=1}^{k} \mathbf{IR}(t-d) \right) \mathbf{u}(t-k) \tag{11}$$

Now, fix t and consider the sequences $\{\alpha_k\}_{k\in[t]} := \mathbf{m}(t-k)$ and $\{\beta_k\}_{k\in[t]} := \prod_{d=1}^{k} \mathbf{IR}(t-d)$. Observe that since $\|\mathbf{IR}(t)\| \leq 1$ we have $\| \prod_{d=0}^{k-1} \mathbf{IR}(t-d)\| \leq \prod_{d=0}^{k-1} \|\mathbf{IR}(t-d)\| \to 0$, as $t, k \to \infty$ thus, $\beta_k \to 0^2$. Further, from the assumptions the α_k is a bounded sequence, so $\sum_k \alpha_k \beta_k \to 0^3$. But $\sum_k \alpha_k \beta_k \to 0$ is the right-hand side of (11). Thus, we conclude. □

Theorem 1 provides a pointwise convergence of $\mathbf{r}(t)$ on $\mathbf{u}(t)$. Also, using Theorem 1 we can deduce the following remark.

Corollary 1. *Consider a Pool game with $|N|$ pools, with a convergent $\mathbf{u}(t)$, and $\mathbf{IR}(t)$ such that $\|\mathbf{IR}(t)\| \leq 1 \, \forall t \in \mathbf{N}$. Then the pool density revenues converges.*

Until now we present the case where every pool at any time step knows the revenue density of all other pools $r_j(t-1)$ and its total infiltration rate $\sum_{j=1}^{p} m_{ji}(t)$. In the following two Subsections we will drop these assumptions and we mitigate the cases where the pools have i) some distribution over the revenue densities, and ii) incorrect revenue densities. Interestingly, as the Pool game is an iterative Prisoner's Dilemma, then it has a dominant equilibrium strategy profile. Thus, in the case where a mediator provides side information to the pools, this will not affect their choices. In a nutshell, a correlation device can not alter the outcome of the Pool game in Table 2 (Fig. 1).

---

[2] It holds, $\lim_{n\to\infty} A^n = 0$ iff the spectral radius of the square matrix A is less than 1, which holds as the spectral radius of a matrix is less or equal than the matrix norm.

[3] Intuitively, we use the fact that if α_k is bounded and if $\beta_k \to 0$, then $\sum_k \alpha_k \beta_k \to 0$.

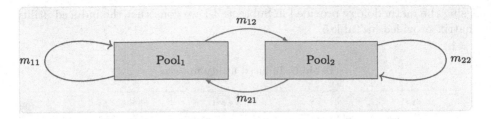

Fig. 1. Pool game with $N = \{\text{Pool}_1, \text{Pool}_2\}$.

4.1 Incomplete Information

From [4] we know that a pool can estimate the rates with which it is attacked. Now, assume that the estimation has a level of uncertainty. E.g., at time t, Pool_2 estimates with probability p_1 that Pool_1 attacks her with the correct infiltration rate $m_{12}(t)$ and with probability p_2 that Pool_1 attacks her with infiltration rate $\hat{m}_{12}(t)$, with $p_1 + p_2 = 1$. At the same time, the Pool_1 does not experience any uncertainty in her estimations, and believes that Pool_2 attacks her with the correct infiltration rate $m_{21}(t)$. Hence, we have a Bayesian game, where Pool_1 has one type $\Theta_{\text{Pool}_1} = \{\theta_{\text{Pool}_1,1}\}$ and Pool_2 has two types $\Theta_{\text{Pool}_2} = \{\theta_{\text{Pool}_2,1}, \theta_{\text{Pool}_2,2}\}$. The density revenues $r_1, r_2, \tilde{r}_1, \tilde{r}_2, r'_1, r'_2, \hat{r}_1$, and $\hat{r}_2$ are compute via the formulas (6)–(8).

Table 3. Information types in Bayesian Pool game with two pools.

Pool$_1$ \ Pool$_2$	attack	non-attack	Pool$_1$ \ Pool$_2$	attack	non-attack
attack	(r_1, r_2)	$(r_1, \tilde{r}_2)$	attack	(r_1, r'_2)	$(r_1, \hat{r}_2)$
non-attack	$(\tilde{r}_1, r_2)$	$(\tilde{r}_1, \tilde{r}_2)$	non-attack	$(\tilde{r}_1, r'_2)$	$(\hat{r}_1, \hat{r}_2)$

(a) Types: $\theta_{\text{Pool}_1,1}, \theta_{\text{Pool}_2,1}$ (b) Types: $\theta_{\text{Pool}_1,1}, \theta_{\text{Pool}_2,2}$

While the utility functions of the pools are given in Table 4.

Table 4. Utility functions u_{Pool_1} and u_{Pool_2} for the Bayesian Pool game from Table 3.

r	c	Θ_{Pool_1}	Θ_{Pool_2}	u_{Pool_1}	u_{Pool_2}
attack	attack	$\theta_{\text{Pool}_1,1}$	$\theta_{\text{Pool}_2,1}$	r_1	r_2
attack	attack	$\theta_{\text{Pool}_1,1}$	$\theta_{\text{Pool}_2,2}$	r'_1	r'_2
attack	non-attack	$\theta_{\text{Pool}_1,1}$	$\theta_{\text{Pool}_2,1}$	$\tilde{r}_1$	r_2
attack	non-attack	$\theta_{\text{Pool}_1,1}$	$\theta_{\text{Pool}_2,2}$	r'_1	$\hat{r}_2$
non-attack	attack	$\theta_{\text{Pool}_1,1}$	$\theta_{\text{Pool}_2,1}$	$\tilde{r}_1$	r_2
non-attack	attack	$\theta_{\text{Pool}_1,1}$	$\theta_{\text{Pool}_2,2}$	$\hat{r}_1$	r'_2
non-attack	non-attack	$\theta_{\text{Pool}_1,1}$	$\theta_{\text{Pool}_2,1}$	$\tilde{r}_1$	$\tilde{r}_2$
non-attack	non-attack	$\theta_{\text{Pool}_1,1}$	$\theta_{\text{Pool}_2,2}$	$\hat{r}_1$	$\hat{r}_2$

Using the methodology provided in Subsect. 3.1 we construct the induced utility matrix provided in Table 5.

Table 5. Induced utility matrix.

	$s_1 s_1$	$s_1 s_2$	$s_2 s_1$	$s_2 s_2$
s_1	$(r_1, p_1 r_2 + p_2 r_2')$	$(r_1, p_1 r_2 + p_2 \hat{r}_2)$	$(r_1, p_1 \tilde{r}_2 + p_2 r_2)$	$(r_1, p_1 \tilde{r}_2 + p_2 \hat{r}_2)$
s_2	$(\tilde{r}_1, p_1 r_2 + p_2 r_2')$	$(\tilde{r}_1, p_1 r_2 + p_2 \hat{r}_2)$	$(\tilde{r}_1, p_1 \tilde{r}_2 + p_2 r_2)$	$(\tilde{r}_1, p_1 \tilde{r}_2 + p_2 \hat{r}_2)$

Next, we can compute the Bayes-Nash equilibria. Then given the finite horizon of the repeated procedure we can derive the final utility for each one of the pools.

Corollary 2. *Consider the Bayesian Pool game BG. If all the utility matrices in the Information types in the BG have constant infiltration rates, then the pool revenues converge.*

For notational convention, let $\mathbf{IR}^i(t)$ be the infiltration matrix, and $\mathbf{r}^i(t)$ be the revenues density, in the ith Information type. Then, the Lemma 1 and Theorem 1 can be transfused in the case of Bayesian Pool games. Namely,

Lemma 2. *Consider a Bayesian Pool game BG with $|N|$ pools. If for all Information types $i \in \Theta$ in the BG, $m_j^i(t)$, $m_{jk}^i(t)$ are non-zero polynomials of equal degree $d \in \mathbb{N}$ with non-negative coefficients $\forall i, j \in [|N|]$ and $\forall t \in \mathbb{N}$, then the pool density revenues converge.*

Proof. From Lemma 1 in each $\mathbf{r}^i(t)$ and the distribution p over the Θs we have that $\lim_{t \to \infty} \mathbf{r}(t) = \lim_{t \to +\infty} \sum_i p_i \mathbf{r}^i(t)$ that converges.   □

Corollary 3. *Consider a Bayesian Pool game BG with $|N|$ pools. If for all Information types $i \in \Theta$ in the BG, $\mathbf{u}^i(t)$ converge, and $\mathbf{IR}^i(t)$ are such that $\|\mathbf{IR}^i(t)\| \leq 1$ $\forall t \in \mathbb{N}$, then the pool revenues converge.*

4.2   Incorrect Information

In the previous Subsection we presented the case where the pools experience uncertainty over the density revenues. Now, assume that the pools have incorrect information regarding the mining power and the density revenues. E.g., at time t, Pool_1 knows the Pool game in Table 6b and the Pool_2 knows the Pool game in Table 6c, whereas the actual situation captured by Table 6a. This is a case of incorrect information and is described by the misinformed Pool game mG with density revenues matrices as provided in Table 6.

Table 6. Misinformed Pool game.

	s_1	s_2
s_1	(r_1, r_2)	$(r_1, \tilde{r}_2)$
s_2	$(\tilde{r}_1, r_2)$	$(\tilde{r}_1, \tilde{r}_2)$

(a) Actual Game

	s_1	s_2
s_1	$(\dot{r}_1, \dot{r}_2)$	$(\dot{r}_1, \hat{r}_2)$
s_2	$(\hat{r}_1, \dot{r}_2)$	$(\hat{r}_1, \hat{r}_2)$

(b) Pool$_1$ game

	s_1	s_2
s_1	$(\bar{r}_1, \bar{r}_2)$	$(\bar{r}_1, \hat{r}'_2)$
s_2	$(\hat{r}'_1, \bar{r}_2)$	$(\hat{r}'_1, \hat{r}'_2)$

(c) Pool$_2$ game

From the analysis of Sect. 4 at each time step each pool will solve independently the system (9). Namely,

$$\text{Pool}_1 : \begin{cases} \dfrac{\partial \hat{r}_1(m^1_{12}(t), m^1_{21}(t))}{\partial m^1_{12}(t)} = 0 \\ \dfrac{\partial \hat{r}_2(m^1_{12}(t), m^1_{21}(t))}{\partial m^1_{21}(t)} = 0 \end{cases}, \quad \text{Pool}_2 : \begin{cases} \dfrac{\partial \hat{r}'_1(m^2_{12}(t), m^2_{21}(t))}{\partial m^2_{12}(t)} = 0 \\ \dfrac{\partial \hat{r}'_2(m^2_{12}(t), m^2_{21}(t))}{\partial m^2_{21}(t)} = 0 \end{cases}$$

(12)

Then the agglomeration of the solution $m^1_{12}(t)$, from the left system, and $m^2_{21}(t)$ from the right system, will provide the *nme*. Given the *nme*, the Adaptation Procedure will evaluate the information of the pools and then the procedure will proceed to the next time step. Thus, the matrices as given in Table 7.

Table 7. Misinformed Pool game after the first step of the Adaptation Procedure.

	s_1	s_2
s_1	(r_1, r_2)	$(r_1, \tilde{r}_2)$
s_2	$(\tilde{r}_1, r_2)$	$(\tilde{r}_1, \tilde{r}_2)$

(a) Actual Game

	s_1	s_2
s_1	(r_1, r_2)	$(\dot{r}_1, \tilde{r}_2)$
s_2	$(\hat{r}_1, \dot{r}_2)$	$(\tilde{r}_1, \hat{r}_2)$

(b) Pool$_1$ game

	s_1	s_2
s_1	(r_1, r_2)	$(\bar{r}_1, \hat{r}'_2)$
s_2	$(\hat{r}'_1, \bar{r}_2)$	$(\tilde{r}_1, \hat{r}'_2)$

(c) Pool$_2$ game

Since all the games in mG are Prisoner's Dilemmas, the Adaptation procedure will update the (*attack − attack*) joint decision according the utilities of the actual game, and will provide $\mathcal{AD}^{(1)}(M)$, that is the misinformed Pool game for the $t = 1$. Observe, that the ordering between r_1 and $\hat{r}_1$, $\hat{r}'_1$, and r_2 and $\tilde{r}_2$, $\hat{r}'_2$ affects the progress of the Adaptation Procedure. Namely,

Corollary 4. *Given the misinformation game in Table 6, if $r_1 > \max\{\hat{r}_1, \hat{r}'_1\}$ and $r_2 > \max\{\hat{r}_2, \hat{r}'_2\}$ then $\mathcal{AD}^{(1)}(M) = \mathcal{AD}^{(0)}(M)$, and the Adaptation Procedure terminates in one step.*

In case the Corollary 4 holds, the misinformed Pool game has a unique *sme*, that is (*attack, attack*). On the other hand,

Lemma 3. *Given the misinformation game in Table 6, if $r_1 < \max\{\hat{r}_1, \hat{r}'_1\}$ or $r_2 < \max\{\hat{r}_2, \hat{r}'_2\}$ then the Adaptation Procedure terminates at most in $|S|$ steps.*

Proof. From Proposition 4.11 in [14] we have that the Adaptation Procedure in the misinformed Pool game Table 6 is finite. It is easy to see that at most the Adaptation Procedure will update the total number of the joint pure strategies of the misinformed game, that is $|S|$. $\square$

In case where the Adaptation Procedure updates all the joint pure strategies of the subjective Pool games, then we end up with a unique *sme*, that is $(attack, attack)$. In any intermediate situation where the Adaptation Procedure terminates in time steps either $t = 2$ or $t = 3$, we need more information in order to conclude about the *smes*.

Next, we have the following results regarding the convergence of the density revenues. We start with the case where the infiltration rates are constant in all games in the misinformation game.

Lemma 4. *Consider the finite misinformation Pool game mG with constant infiltration rates for all $G^i s$ and G^0, then the pool density revenues converge.*

Proof. From the Corollary 4 and Lemma 3 the Adaptation Procedure terminates. Then, from Lemma 1 in [4] we conclude.   □

Abusing notation, we denote as $\mathbf{u}^0$, $\mathbf{u}^i$ the direct mining revenue densities, and m_{ij}^0, m_{ij}^i are the infiltration rates in the actual game G^0 and in the G^i respectively.

Lemma 5. *Consider the finite misinformation Pool game mG, then if $m_j^i(t)$, $m_{jk}^i(t)$ are non-zero polynomials of equal degree $d \in \mathbb{N}$ with non-negative coefficients $\forall i, j \in [|N|]$ and $\forall t \in \mathbb{N}$, then the pool density revenues converge.*   □

Proof. Using Lemma 1 for each G^i we have that each $\mathbf{r}^i(t)$ converges. Further, from Lemma 3 the Adaptation Procedure for mG terminates in finite time, thus the revenue densities converge for the mG.

Lemma 6. *Consider the finite misinformation Pool game mG, $\mathbf{u}^i(t)$ are bounded, and $\mathbf{IR}^i(t)$ are such that $\|\mathbf{IR}^i(t)\| \leq 1 \ \forall t \in \mathbb{N}$, then the pool revenues converge.*

Proof. Using Theorem 1 for each G^i we have that each $\mathbf{r}^i(t)$ converges. Further, from Lemma 3 the Adaptation Procedure for mG terminates in finite time, thus the revenue densities converge for the mG.   □

Interestingly, we can attain convergence of the density revenues of the mG in the case where the subjective games G^i have general infiltration rates. This is provided by te following result.

Corollary 5. *Consider the finite misinformation Pool game mG, such that $\mathbf{u}^0(t) > \mathbf{u}^i(t)$, $\forall i \in [|N|]$ and the Adaptation Procedure terminates after $|S|$ steps. If one of the following holds*

– *the infiltration rates of the G^0 are constant*
– *the $m_i^0(t)$, and $m_{ij}^0(t)$ are non-zero polynomials with non-negative coefficients of equal degree $\forall i \in [|N|]$*
– *$\forall t$ the $\mathbf{u}^0(t)$ converges and $\|\mathbf{IR}^0(t)\| \leq 1$*

Then the density revenues for the mG converge.

In the case where the assumptions of the Corollary 5 hold then $SME(mG) = \{\sigma | \ \sigma := (\sigma_1, \ldots, \sigma_{|N|}), \ \sigma_i \in ne_j \text{ for some } ne_j \in NE(G^0)\}$. In other words, the *sme*'s of the mG are all the combinations of the Nash equilibria strategy profiles of the pools in G^0.

5   Numerical Experiments

The theoretical results of Sect. 4 cope with the Pool game in various information environments. Here, we empirically demonstrate the evolution of the density revenues of the Pool game, as provided by the equation $\mathbf{r}^*(t) = \mathbf{u}^*(t) + \mathbf{IR}^*(t) \cdot \mathbf{r}^*(t-1)$ analyzed in Sect. 4[4], considering the cases of i) complete and correct information, ii) incomplete information, and iii) incorrect information. In what follows $T = 1000$, the number of pools is $|N| = 2$, where each one starts with 100 miners. As shown in Table 8 the number of miners does not remain constant. Further, we take $\mathbf{r}(0) = (m_{12}^*(0), m_{21}^*(0))^T$ for all cases.

To demonstrate our numerical results we use the functions provided in Table 8. More specifically, we use linear functions (second column) to study the case where pools attract miners that increase proportionally in time. Second, we pick cubic functions (third column) as they are "relatively simple" polynomial functions that experience critical points. Apparently, the properties of the functions affect the behavior of the pools.

Table 8. Polynomial functions for $m(t)$s.

	Figs. 2a, 3a, 3b, 4a, 4b	Figs. 2b, 3c, 3d, 4c, 4d
$m_1(t)$	$200t + 100$	$6t^3 + 10t^2 + 4t + 100$
$m_{11}(t)$	$110t + (100 - m_{12}(0))$	$5t^3 + 7t^2 + t + (100 - m_{12}(0))$
$m_{12}(t)$	$40t + m_{12}(0)$	$4t^3 + 2t^2 + 2t + m_{12}(0)$
$m_2(t)$	$156t + 100$	$8t^3 + 9t^2 + 4t + 100$
$m_{21}(t)$	$20t + m_{21}(0)$	$3t^3 + 3t^2 + 2t + m_{21}(0)$
$m_{22}(t)$	$91t + (100 - m_{21}(0))$	$4t^3 + 5t^2 + t + (100 - m_{21}(0))$

Complete - Correct Information. In this case, the pools have complete and correct information regarding the Pool game. In Figs. 2a, 2b we compute the density revenues with initial values $m_{11}(0) = 60$, $m_{12}(0) = 40$, $m_{21}(0) = 10$, and $m_{22}(0) = 90$. Further, the density revenue functions for the case where the $m(t)$s are provided by Table 8.

Incomplete Information. For the case of incomplete information we provide experiments both for the undiscounted and the discounted cases, as they were presented in Subsect. 3.1, whereas we compute the density rates, using the settings in Table 9. In Figs. 3 are shown both the undiscounted (Figs. 3a, 3c) and the discounted cases (Figs. 3b, 3d). Further, in Figs. 3a, 3b, 3c, and 3d the $m(t)$s are polynomial functions and are provided by Table 8. Clearly, the numerical results are inline with Lemma 2, and Corollaries 2, and 3.

---

[4] The asterisk refers to the different information environments.

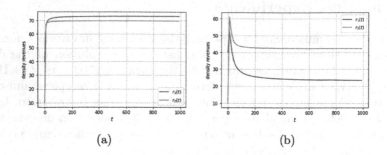

(a)   (b)

Fig. 2. Realisations for the density revenues for the complete-correct information environment.

Table 9. Initial infiltration rates, distribution over Information sets, and δ.

Case	$m_{11}(0)$	$m_{12}(0)$	$m_{21}(0)$	$m_{22}(0)$	p	δ
Undiscounted	90	10	30	70	.4	-
	60	40	40	60	.6	
Discounted	90	10	30	70	.4	.8
	60	40	40	60	.6	

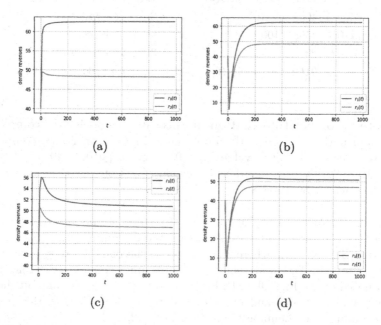

(a)   (b)

(c)   (d)

Fig. 3. Realisations for the density revenues regarding incomplete information environment, see Table 9.

Incorrect Information. The pools have subjective views regarding the Pool game. This case is analysed using misinformation games, as presented in Subsect. 3.2 for the values of Table 10. The asterisk in Table 10 simply implies that these values are according to the game in the second column.

In Figs. 4a–4d we compute the density revenues as provided by the equations (12), using polynomial infiltration rates, see Figs. 4a, 4b, 4c, and 4d. Since all the actual and the subjective Pool games are in the class of Prisoners' Dilemma the misinformed Pool game has a unique nme. So, the Adaptation procedure will terminate in one step. Observe that eventually, the density revenues converge to the values close to the density revenues in the case of complete-correct information. This happens because $m(t)$s are increasing functions and masking the effect of the update. Thus, the structure of $m(t)$s can tune the effect of misinformation. Finally, the numerical results are in line with Lemmas 4, 5, and 6.

Table 10. Initial infiltration rates for a misinformed Pool game.

Game	$m_{11}(0)$	$m_{12}(0)$	$m_{21}(0)$	$m_{22}(0)$
Actual	60	40	20	80
G^{Pool_1}	70	30	20	80
G^{Pool_2}	90	10	40	60

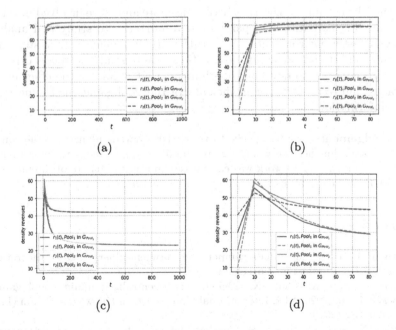

(a)

(b)

(c)

(d)

Fig. 4. Realisations for the density revenues regarding the settings that presented in Table 10, for the incorrect information environment.

As a general remark, $m(t)$s influence the density revenues. In cases where $r(t)$ attain a critical point, the pools may have incentives to stop/continue the interaction. For example, in Fig. 2b the pools attain the maximum density revenues early in time. On the other hand, in Fig. 3b the pools attain the minimum density revenues early and then they recover. As a result, the pools can exploit the properties of $m(t)$s for their benefit.

6   Conclusions

In this paper, we transfuse and study the Pool game model, which was introduced in [4], under different information environments. In particular, we consider the cases where the pools i) experience uncertainty, and ii) have erroneous information regarding the interaction. We provide theoretical results regarding the convergence of the density revenues in all cases, and we generalize the convergence results in [4]. In parallel, we demonstrate experimentally the theoretical results in all the aforementioned information environments.

Our analysis provides several insights regarding the behavior of the pools. First, we show experimentally, for all information environments, that the behavior of the pools is affected severely by the formulas of infiltration rates. In that direction, if the formulas are linear then we can expect the Pool game to converge quicker compared to the case of cubic formulas. Second in case of incorrect information the pools are not necessarily to understand the actual interaction in order to converge.

As the Blockchain framework is becoming more and more involved in versatile and demanding activities is of paramount importance to study and analyze it in more realistic environments. With this work, we make a first step in this direction. To that end, some future directions are to study protocols other than withholding attacks, to develop a mechanism that regulates the efficiency of a Pool game, and to measure the inefficiency of the Pool game due to uncertainty, and misinformation.

Acknowledgements. We would like to thank Dr. Giorgos Flouris for the constructive suggestions. Further, we would like to thank the anonymous reviewers for their productive comments. This work was carried out during the tenure of the first author in an ERCIM 'Alain Bensoussan' Fellowship Programme.

References

1. Altman, E., et al.: Blockchain competition between miners: a game theoretic perspective. In: Frontiers in Blockchain (2020)
2. Chen, Z., Sun, X., Shan, X., Zhang, J.: Decentralized mining pool games in blockchain. In: 2020 IEEE International Conference on Knowledge Graph (ICKG), pp. 426–432 (2020)
3. Deepa, N., et al.: A survey on blockchain for big data: approaches, opportunities, and future directions. Future Gener. Comput. Syst. **131**, 209–226 (2020)

4. Eyal, I.: The miner's dilemma. In: 2015 IEEE Symposium on Security and Privacy, pp. 89–103 (2014)
5. Huang, H., Kong, W., Zhou, S., Zheng, Z., Guo, S.: A survey of state-of-the-art on blockchains: Theories, modelings, and tools. arXiv:2007.03520 (2020)
6. Juhász, P., Stéger, J., Kondor, D., Vattay, G.: A Bayesian approach to identify bitcoin users. PLoS ONE. **13**, e0207000 (2016)
7. Kiayias, A., Koutsoupias, E., Kyropoulou, M., Tselekounis, Y.: Blockchain mining games. In: Proceedings of the 2016 ACM Conference on Economics and Computation, EC 2016, pp. 365–382 (2016)
8. Lewenberg, Y., Bachrach, Y., Sompolinsky, Y., Zohar, A., Rosenschein, J.S.: Bitcoin mining pools: a cooperative game theoretic analysis. In: Proceedings of the 2015 International Conference on Autonomous Agents and Multiagent Systems, AAMAS 2015, pp. 919–927 (2015)
9. Leyton-Brown, K., Shoham, Y.: Essentials of Game Theory: A Concise Multidisciplinary Introduction. Synthesis Lectures on Artificial Intelligence and Machine Learning, pp. 1–88. Springer Nature, Switzerland (2008). https://doi.org/10.1007/978-3-031-01545-8
10. Li, W., Cao, M., Wang, Y., Tang, C., Lin, F.: Mining pool game model and Nash equilibrium analysis for pow-based blockchain networks. IEEE Access **8**, 101049–101060 (2020)
11. Liu, Z., et al.: A survey on applications of game theory in blockchain. arXiv:1902.10865 (2019)
12. Nakamoto, S.: Bitcoin: A peer-to-peer electronic cash system (2008)
13. Nash, J.F.: Non-cooperative games. Ann. Math. 286–295 (1951)
14. Papamichail, M., Varsos, C., Flouris, G.: Implementing the adaptation procedure in misinformation games. In: Proceedings of the 12th Hellenic Conference on Artificial Intelligence (2022)
15. Shi, Z., Zhou, H., de Laat, C.T.A.M., Zhao, Z.G.: A Bayesian game-enhanced auction model for federated cloud services using blockchain. Future Gener. Comput, Syst. **136**, 49-66 (2022)
16. Varsos, C., Flouris, G., Bitsaki, M., Fasoulakis, M.: A study of misinformation games. In: Pacific Rim International Conference on Artificial Intelligence (2021)
17. Wu, D.A., dong Liu, X., Yan, X., Peng, R., Li, G.: Equilibrium analysis of bitcoin block withholding attack: a generalized model. Reliab. Eng. Syst. Saf. **185**, 318–328 (2019)
18. Zappalà, P., Belotti, M., Potop-Butucaru, M.G., Secci, S.: Brief announcement: game theoretical framework for analyzing blockchains robustness. In: International Symposium on Distributed Computing (2020)
19. Zhao, Z., Chen, X., Zhou, Y.: Bayesian-Nash-incentive-compatible mechanism for blockchain transaction fee allocation. arXiv:2209.13099 (2022)

Mixed Technologies

Operating with Quantum Integers: An Efficient 'Multiples of' Oracle

Javier Sanchez-Rivero[1]([✉]), Daniel Talaván[1], Jose Garcia-Alonso[2],
Antonio Ruiz-Cortés[3], and Juan Manuel Murillo[1,2]

[1] COMPUTAEX, Cáceres, Spain
jszrivero@gmail.com
[2] University of Extremadura, Cáceres, Spain
[3] Universidad de Sevilla, Sevilla, Spain

Abstract. Quantum algorithms are a very promising field. However, creating and manipulating these kind of algorithms is a very complex task, specially for software engineers used to work at higher abstraction levels. The work presented here is part of a broader research focused on providing operations of a higher abstraction level to manipulate integers codified as a superposition. These operations are designed to be composable and efficient, so quantum software developers can reuse them to create more complex solutions. Specifically, in this paper we present a 'multiples of' operation. To validate this operation, we show several examples of quantum circuits and their simulations, including its composition possibilities. A theoretical analysis proves that both the complexity of the required classical calculations and the depth of the circuit scale linearly with the number of qubits. Hence, the 'multiples of' oracle is efficient in terms of complexity and depth. Finally, an empirical study of the circuit depth is conducted to further reinforce the theoretical analysis.

Keywords: Quantum computing · Amplitude Amplification · Oracle · Multiples · Qiskit

1 Introduction

Quantum computing [17] uses quantum mechanics to perform computations in a different manner than classical computing [18]. Nowadays, quantum computers are in the NISQ (Noisy Intermediate-Scale Quantum) Era [19], which means their practical use is still limited by errors and the low number of qubits (quantum bits). However, the recent developments on quantum devices have allowed researchers to start testing on real quantum hardware the theoretical work on quantum algorithms, which has been a very active field for decades [12].

Quantum algorithms are useful when they can solve certain problems faster than any known classical algorithm [16]. This speedup is measured in terms of asymptotic scaling of complexity [4]. The work presented here is part of ongoing

M. Aiello et al. (Eds.): SummerSOC 2023, CCIS 1847, pp. 105–124, 2023.
https://doi.org/10.1007/978-3-031-45728-9_7

research aimed at providing programmers with operations on quantum states at a higher level of abstraction than the base quantum gates. The design of these operations aims at composability and efficiency, such that they can be reused to create larger solutions. More specifically, our research has begun with the goal of providing operations on a superposition quantum state that encodes integers with size determined by the number of qubits in the state [20]. These operations are not only useful for manipulating a quantum state encoding integers, they are also more efficient than the same operations in the classical domain. In addition, the quantum circuits that implement these operations are optimised in depth, with respect to Qiskit's automatic methods [23], as well as in the number of qubits (ancilla and non-ancilla) they use [21].

In particular, this paper presents an operation that computes multiples. Thus, given an integer and a quantum state that encodes integers, the operation phase-tags[1] the configurations of the quantum state that correspond to multiples of the given integer. While the complexity of finding the multiples in the classical domain is $\mathcal{O}(2^{n_N})$,[2] the complexity of the operation presented here is $\mathcal{O}(n_N)$, where n_N is the number of bits codifying the maximum size of the wanted multiples, N. This is a logarithmic scaling in the total number of states, which provides an exponential speedup with respect to classical calculations.

As mentioned before, in our research this 'multiples of' is part of a larger set of quantum operations on integers [20,21]. An important feature that we want the whole set of operations to preserve is composability. Thus, all the resources of this set are composable with each other and, for example, the 'multiples of' can be composed with a 'less than' operation to obtain the multiples of a given integer a less than another given integer b. In particular, the operation 'multiples of' can also be composed with itself to, for example, mark in a quantum state the multiples of an integer a and then, in the resulting state, mark the multiples of another integer b. Preserving composability offers the possibility to reuse such operations to build more complex operations with a higher level of abstraction. Achieving the best quality attributes, such as reusability or composability, in each operation is important because their compositions will inherit those attributes [14,24].

This paper is organized as follows. In Sect. 2 we provide the necessary background for this work. Next, the description of the 'multiples of' operation is presented in Sect. 4. The operation takes the shape of a quantum oracle and the section details both the idea inspiring the oracle and the quantum circuit exact implementation. In Sect. 5 some examples of circuits and simulations are shown to prove the functionality of the oracle. Then, in Sect. 6, the complexity of classical calculations as well as the quantum circuit is discussed. Section 7 shows composability and further uses of the oracle. Finally, in Sect. 8, the conclusions and future work are explored.

---

[1] Phase-tagging a state is giving that state a π-phase.
[2] Given $k \in \mathbb{N}$, there are $\lceil N/k \rceil$ multiples of k in $[0, N]$. As k is fixed, the number of multiples grows linearly in N, $\mathcal{O}(N)$. Namely, if $N = 2^{n_N}$, then $\mathcal{O}(2^{n_N})$.

2   Background

Oracles have been identified as a recurring pattern in quantum software [15,24]. Following this trend, the work presented here is built as an oracle for Grover's algorithm [9]. This algorithm searches for one quantum state in an unordered database faster than any known classical algorithm. Its generalization is called Amplitude Amplification [3,10] and allows to search for multiple values. This algorithm works by applying two quantum operations: an oracle, which marks with a π-phase the desired quantum states, and a diffuser, which tries to amplify the amplitude of those marked states. Often, to reach a satisfactory amplification, it is needed to repeat the pair oracle-diffuser several times. This pair oracle-diffuser is usually called the Grover iterator.

The 'multiples of' oracle is built reusing two pieces of existing quantum software, the linear multi-controlled gate [22] and the modulo addition [1,7].

In [22] the authors present an efficient implementation of a multi-controlled gate whose depth scales linearly with the number of qubits and thus avoids the polynomial growth of previous implementations. Furthermore, it does not require the use of ancilla qubits. The linear multi-control gate outperforms Qiskit [23] implementation from five qubits onwards, which supposes a clear improvement for any meaningful use. Furthermore, the authors also conduct an analysis on the utility of the linear multi-controlled gate on NISQ devices, showing that the depth reduction can help achieve more accurate results. Because of these quality attributes, we chose to reuse it in this work.

The modulo addition operation $a + b$ mod k is defined as the remainder of dividing $a + b$ by k. In this work, this operation will only be performed with values $a, b < k$. Hence, in our case, the modulo addition can be written as:

$$a + b \bmod k = \begin{cases} a + b & \text{if } a + b < k \\ a + b - k & \text{if } a + b \geq k \end{cases} \quad a, b < k \tag{1}$$

For this modulo addition we use the implementation presented in [1]. It is heavily based on Draper's algorithm [7] for quantum addition. This method uses the quantum Fourier transform [6] and hence is done on the frequency domain[3]. It allows the addition of an integer to a quantum superposed state without the need to encode the integer in a quantum register. This reduces the number of necessary qubits. The depth of this operation is linear on the number of qubits, as it is a composition of linear-depth primitives.

Once the addition gate is built, the modulo addition conducts the following operations [1]: adds a classical value $a < k$ to a quantum state holding the classical value $b < k$, and then it subtracts k if $a + b \geq k$. This methods requires two ancilla qubits to perform the operation, one for the overflowing of the sum, and another one for checking whether it is needed to subtract k or not.

---

[3] In the frequency domain, integers are represented by superposition of states with the same different in phase between the state. That difference in phase is the unique identifier of the integer [18].

This paper showcases how by carefully composing existing pieces of quantum software a new non-trivial software can be obtained. The ideas hereby described are the ones which allow to build the oracle 'multiples of', presented in detail in Sect. 4.

3   Related Works

There are several approaches which seek to create higher-level quantum programming languages. Quipper [8] is a scalable quantum programming language which can be used to program several quantum algorithms, such as HHL [11]. Silq [2] is a high-level quantum language which focuses, among other objectives, in the automatic uncomputation of operations usually required in quantum programming. Another construction of higher-level quantum program is Classiq [5], which researches in building oracles for arithmetic expressions. Latter one is the closest to our work, previous ones focus on quantum primitives with a more general approach. Operations in Classiq, range from addition or subtraction to built-in functions such as Amplitude Estimation. These languages aim at creating a whole set of operations to be able to create quantum software without the need of deep knowledge on quantum circuits. Our work follows the same idea and attempts to create new more complex operations with efficient classical calculations.

4   Implementation of the 'Multiples of' Oracle

In this section, we provide a description of the oracle. It comprises two differentiated parts, the first one is the mathematical ideas inspiring the oracle, where basic modulo theory shows a condition for identifying multiples. The second part describes the quantum circuit of the oracle, how the multiples are given a π-phase, and how to adapt the oracle for a full Amplitude Amplification implementation.

4.1   Mathematical Properties Inspiring the Oracle

A number $M \in \mathbb{N}$ is multiple of another number k if the remainder of the division is 0, formally expressed as $M \equiv 0 \bmod k$. If M is not a multiple of k, then $M \not\equiv 0 \bmod k$.

The number M can be be expressed in binary form, also known as binary decomposition:

$$M = a_m \cdot 2^m + a_{m-1} \cdot 2^{m-1} + \ldots + a_1 \cdot 2^1 + a_0 \cdot 2^0 = \sum_{i=0}^{m} a_i \cdot 2^i \qquad (2)$$

where $a_i \in \{0, 1\}$ and $m = \lceil \log_2 M \rceil$.

Let r_i, with $0 \leq r_i < k$, be the remainder of 2^i when divided by k, formally:

$$2^i \equiv r_i \bmod k \tag{3}$$

Then by the properties of the ring of remainders $\mathbb{Z}_k$ it can be noticed that:

$$M \equiv \sum_{i=0}^{m} a_i \cdot 2^i \equiv \sum_{i=0}^{m} a_i \cdot r_i \bmod k \tag{4}$$

Hence, M is a multiple of k if the sum of the remainders of the powers of 2 modulo k of its binary decomposition is equivalent to 0, formally:

$$M \equiv 0 \bmod k \iff \sum_{i=0}^{m} a_i \cdot r_i \equiv 0 \bmod k \tag{5}$$

Therefore, the 'multiples of' oracle is built in two parts, first adding the remainders of the powers of two, and then giving a π-phase to those which are 0, thus the multiples.

4.2 Algorithm for the 'Multiples of' Oracle

This subsection provides a detailed explanation of the implementation of the 'multiples of' oracle.

Let $k \in \mathbb{N}$ be the number whose multiples want to be calculated. The quantum circuit for the 'multiples of k' oracle consists of three registers of qubits.

The first is the input register, which holds the quantum states in which the multiples will be searched. It is formed by n qubits and the i-th qubit of this register is denoted q_i. The number n is an input parameter and does not depend on any other value. Thus, the numbers in which the multiples will be searched range from 0 to $N - 1$, where $N = 2^n$.

The second register holds the remainder of the numbers. At most, the remainder of dividing by k is $k - 1$, hence the required number of qubits for this register is $n_k = \lceil \log_2(k - 1) \rceil$. The i-th qubit of this register is denoted rq_i.

Finally, an ancilla register with two qubits is needed to perform the modulo addition introduced in the Sect. 2, as described in detail in [1]. These qubits are denoted ancilla$_0$ and ancilla$_1$. Both the registers and the ancilla registers are initialized to state $|0\rangle$.

Algorithm 1 builds the circuit. It follows an explanation which describes it thoroughly.

The remainders of each power of 2, $r_i \equiv 2^i \bmod k$, are added modulo k to the remainders register, where the addition is controlled by the input qubit q_i. As the remainders register is initialized as $|0\rangle$ and $r_i < k \ \forall i$, the result of each modulo addition will never be larger than k, as shown in the definition of this operation in Sect. 2. Figure 1 shows the general case of this implementation. This image and all the others showing circuits have been done with the *quantikz* package [13].

Data: Number of qubits n and a natural number k
Result: Quantum Circuit which gives a π-phase to all states representing
        binary forms of natural numbers multiples of k
Calculate $r_i \equiv 2^i \bmod k$ for $i \in [0, n-1]$;   `/* see Appendix A */`
$n_k \leftarrow \lceil \log_2(k-1) \rceil$;
input_register $(q) \leftarrow QuantumRegister(n)$;
remainder_register $(rq) \leftarrow QuantumRegister(n_k)$;
ancilla_register $\leftarrow QuantumRegister(2)$;
$n_{total} \leftarrow n + n_k + 2$;
$circ \leftarrow QuantumCircuit(n_{total})$;
Initialize input_register to $|0\rangle$;
for $i = 0$ **to** $n-1$ **do**
   | $circ^+ = ModuloAddition(r_i, n_k + 2)$;
   | append $circ^+$ to $circ$:
   | - Target: remainder_register and ancilla_register;
   | - Control: q_i;
end
for $j = 0$ **to** $n_k - 1$ **do**
   | X gate to rq_j;
end
CZ^{n_k} gate to qubits $rq_0, \ldots, rq_{n_k-1}$;
;   `/* Target: `rq_{n_k-1}`, Control: `$rq_0, \ldots, rq_{n_k-2}$` */`
for $j = 0$ **to** $n_k - 1$ **do**
   | X gate to rq_j;
end
for $i = 0$ **to** $n-1$ **do**
   | $circ^- = ModuloSubstraction(r_i, n_k + 2)$;
   | append $circ^-$ to $circ$:
   | - Target: remainder_register and ancilla_register;
   | - Control: q_i;
end

Algorithm 1: Algorithm for building the 'multiples of' oracle

After applying the modulo additions, the ancilla register is always at state $|00\rangle$ [1]. The remainders register holds states from $|0\rangle$ up to $|k-1\rangle$. From Eq. 5, it can be seen that the multiples of k are those states of the form:

$$|rq_{n_k-1} \ldots rq_1\, rq_0\, q_{n-1} \ldots q_1\, q_0\rangle = |\; \underbrace{0 \ldots 0\, 0}_{rq \text{ register}}\; \underbrace{q_{n-1} \ldots q_1\, q_0}_{\text{input register}}\rangle \qquad (6)$$

Hence, these states and only these ones will be given a π-phase by means of the gate 7:

$$X^{\otimes n_k} \cdot CZ^{n_k} \cdot X^{\otimes n_k} \qquad (7)$$

where CZ^{n_k} is a multi-controlled Z-gate whose target is qubit rq_{n_k-1} and controlled by qubits $rq_0, \ldots, rq_{n_k-2}$. This gate is built using the linear multi-controlled Z-gate introduced in Sect. 2. Figure 2 shows how this part of the circuit is built.

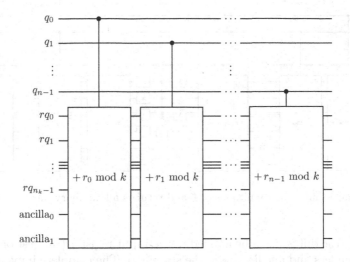

Fig. 1. Modulo addition of the remainders of the powers of 2.

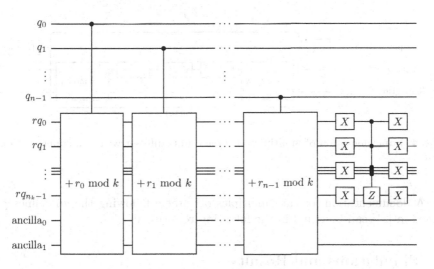

Fig. 2. Oracle that marks multiples of k.

Afterwards, in order to apply the diffuser, it is required to return auxiliary qubits to their initial states, that is, to perform an uncomputation on this register [18]. As the multiples are already given a π-phase, if the modulo additions of the remainders are uncomputed, the states would keep the phase. The circuit would be as in Fig. 3.

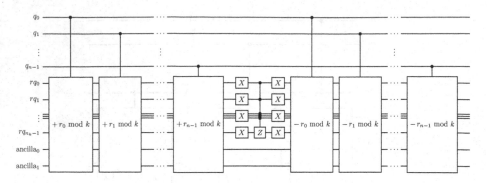

Fig. 3. Oracle that marks multiples of k and returns all auxiliary qubits to state $|0\rangle$.

Finally, the diffuser can be applied to the input register (the rest of the registers, remainders and ancilla, are in the state $|0\rangle$). The complete implementation is shown in Fig. 4.

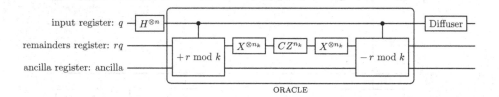

Fig. 4. Implementation of 'multiples of' oracle plus diffuser with full superposition as input.

A documentation for this 'multiples of' oracle following the guidelines proposed in [21] can be found in the following repository.

5   Simulations and Results

In this section, we show some examples of the oracle, both the implementations and the results, which are obtained by means of a simulator with no noise and no error model applied. Different values for k, the number whose multiples are calculated, and n, the number of input qubits[4], are chosen to showcase the functionality of the 'multiples of' oracle. We display the full circuit for the multiples of 3 oracle with 4 qubits input as well as its simulation. We also show the full circuit and the simulation of multiples of 5 with 6 qubits. We have chosen these values for k and number of input qubits to improve readability of the circuits.

---

[4] We codify all our integers as quantum states in these n qubits, hence the multiples are calculated up to $N = 2^n$ integers.

In addition, we also show a simulation of multiples of 14 with 5 qubits using one and two repetitions of the Grover iterator to showcase the difference in the amplified amplitude in both cases.

We have used Qiskit [23] to generate the circuits and simulate them. To be able to amplify the marked quantum states we have chosen a full superposition of 0s and 1s as our input state and have applied the Grover's algorithm diffuser [18] after the oracle. All the simulations are conducted with 20,000 shots[5] as it is the maximum allowed by Qiskit.

5.1   Multiples of 3

The 'multiples of 3' oracle with 4 qubits as input can be found in Fig. 5. The remainders of the powers of 2 when divided by 3 follow the cycle 1, 2, as:

$$2^0 \equiv 1 \bmod 3$$
$$2^1 \equiv 2 \bmod 3 \qquad (8)$$
$$2^2 \equiv 1 \bmod 3$$

As there are 4 input qubits, the remainders of the first 4 powers of 2 are added in the remainders register. These 4 remainders are 1, 2, 1, 2, repeating the whole cycle once.

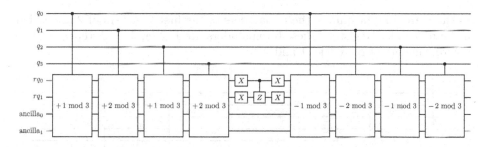

Fig. 5. Multiples of 3 oracle with a 4 qubits input register.

The result of simulating the entire circuit, including the initialisation of the state, the shown oracle, and the diffuser, are shown on Fig. 6. The x-axis represents the final quantum states and the y-axis represents the relative frequency. Desired states (multiples of 3) are in blue with a thick border, undesired states (not multiples of 3) are in red without border. It can be noticed that with just one repetition, the desired states are clearly amplified to differentiate the multiples of 3 from the rest of the numbers.

---

[5] Each shot is one simulation of the circuit, the final result is the aggregation of all shots.

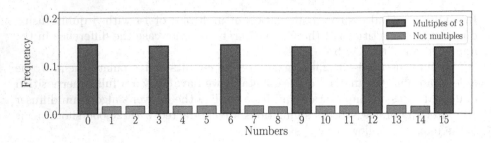

Fig. 6. Results of simulating the circuit of multiples of 3 with a 4 qubits input.

5.2   Multiples of 5

The 'multiples of 5' oracle with 6 qubits as input can be found in Fig. 7. The remainders of the powers of 2 when divided by 5 follow the cycle 1, 2, 4, 3, as:

$$2^0 \equiv 1 \bmod 5$$
$$2^1 \equiv 2 \bmod 5$$
$$2^2 \equiv 4 \bmod 5 \tag{9}$$
$$2^3 \equiv 3 \bmod 5$$
$$2^4 \equiv 1 \bmod 5$$

As there are 6 input qubits, the remainders of the first 6 powers of 2 are added in the remainders register. These 6 remainders are 1, 2, 4, 3, 1, 2, repeating the first remainders of the cycle, 1 and 2.

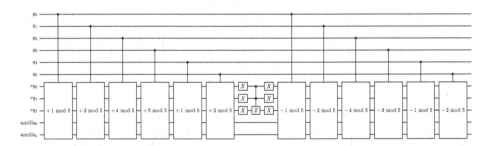

Fig. 7. Multiples of 5 oracle with a 6 qubits input register.

The result of simulating the full circuit, including the initialisation of the state, the shown oracle and the diffuser; are shown on Fig. 8. It can be seen that, in this case, the amplification with one iteration is almost perfect.

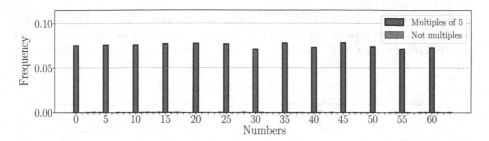

Fig. 8. Results of simulating the circuit of multiples of 5 with a 6 qubits input.

5.3   Multiples of 14

In this section, we show the results of simulating the 'multiples of 14' with 5 input qubits in full superposition with one and two repetitions of the Grover iterator. The remainders of the powers of 2 are 1, 2, 4, 8, and 2. We do not show the circuits for the sake of readability, however they can be found in the provided repository.

Figure 9 shows the results of the simulation using one repetition. The total amount of amplification of desired states is ≈ 64%. Although from an absolute perspective this may not seem a favourable result, the three desired states (0, 14 and 28, multiples of 14 up to 31) have their amplitude enlarged by a factor ≈ 6.82. This amplification allows the distinction of multiples of 14 among the input states.

On Fig. 10 are depicted the results of the simulation using two repetitions. In this case, the total amount of amplification is ≈ 100%. This is the best possible amplification and shows that this oracle may improve its applicability by repeating the pair oracle-diffuser. However, the increased depth of this operation has to be taken into account when implementing the operation in a real quantum device.

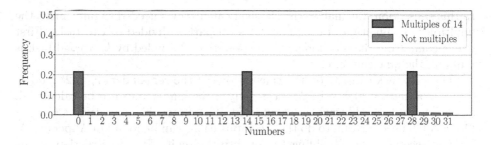

Fig. 9. Results of simulating the circuit of multiples of 14 with a 5 qubits input with one repetition of the Grover iterator.

Knowing the number of desired states, M, and the total number of states, N, the number of repetitions to reach maximum amplification can be calculated exactly [18]. Further analyses on the number of repetitions are conducted in [9] [10].

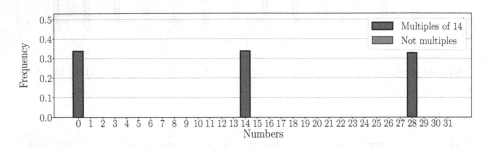

Fig. 10. Results of simulating the circuit of multiples of 14 with a 5 qubits input with two repetitions of the Grover iterator.

6 Complexity and Depth

In this section, we present both an analysis of the classical calculations required to build the quantum oracle and also a theoretical and empirical study of the depth of the resulting quantum oracle.

Let us bear in mind that $k \in \mathbb{N}$ is the number whose multiples want to be calculated; n is the number of input qubits, in which the multiples of k are going to be calculated; $N = 2^n$ is the total number of quantum states; and n_k is the required number of qubits to store the remainders of dividing by k (at most $k - 1$).

6.1 Classical Calculations Complexity

In this subsection, we analyse the classical calculations needed to implement the 'multiples of' quantum oracle. This classical part is divided in two tasks. First one is computing the remainders of the powers of 2 divided by k. Second task is building the quantum circuit.

The first task consists on the calculations of the remainders $r_i \equiv 2^i \bmod k$, $0 \le r_i < k$ and $i \in [0, n-1]$. At most, only n remainders need to be calculated, as only n modulo additions are conducted. Therefore, this operation is $\mathcal{O}(n) = \mathcal{O}(\log N)$. The algorithm to do these computations can be found in Appendix A.

The second task is building the quantum circuit. The construction of the controlled circuit '$+r \bmod k$' which performs the modulo addition is linear on the number of qubits [1]. In this case, the number of qubits on the remainders register, n_k. This means that the complexity of this operation is $\mathcal{O}(\log k) =$

$\mathcal{O}(n_k)$. This is smaller than $\mathcal{O}(n)$, otherwise, k would be greater than $N = 2^n$ and there would be only one multiple in those integers, the number 0.

Moreover, the complexity of appending the modulo addition circuits to the full quantum circuit is linear on the number of qubits on the input register, n, thus, $\mathcal{O}(n) = \mathcal{O}(\log N)$. The rest of needed appends (Hadamard, X and multi-controlled Z) are also linear with the number of qubits. Therefore, the complete procedure required in classical computations holds a complexity of $\mathcal{O}(n) = \mathcal{O}(\log N)$.

It can be noted that for obtaining the multiples of a given number k up to N classically, it is needed to calculate $\lceil N/k \rceil$ multiples. Hence, as k is already fixed, this calculation grows exponentially with the number of binary bits, n_N, needed to encode N in binary form, $\mathcal{O}(N) = \mathcal{O}(2^{n_N})$. To apply our method, we need to encode N in a quantum circuit and n_N qubits are needed. As showed above, the complexity of the classical computations of our method is $\mathcal{O}(n_N)$, hence, our method presents an exponential reduction of the complexity of the classical computations.

6.2 Theoretical Analysis of Quantum Circuit Depth

As stated in Sect. 4.2, the quantum circuit consists of three registers of qubits, the input qubits, which hold the information for all the possible numbers, formed by n qubits, which is input from the user. The register which holds the remainder of the numbers, which has $n_k = \lceil \log_2(k-1) \rceil$ qubits. At most, the remainder of dividing by k is $k - 1$, hence not more qubits are required. Finally, an ancilla register with two qubits is needed to perform the modulo addition, as described in detail in [1]. The depth of this circuit is determined by the depth of its two reused oracles, the modulo addition and the phase-marking operation.

The modulo addition '$+r \mod k$' has linear depth on the number of qubits, in this case $\mathcal{O}(n_k) = \mathcal{O}(\log k)$, as it is applied on the remainders register. Once k is chosen, the depth of this circuit is fixed. This operation needs to be applied $2n$ times, firstly to compute the remainders and afterwards to uncompute them. Therefore, the depth of this operation is $\mathcal{O}(n) = \mathcal{O}(\log N)$.

The phase-marking operation requires a multi-controlled Z-gate. This is implemented following [22], which provides a linear depth on the number of qubits, $\mathcal{O}(n_k) = \mathcal{O}(\log k)$. As stated in the previous Subsect. 6.1, this is upper-bounded by $\mathcal{O}(n)$.

Therefore, the depth of the full implementation of the 'multiples of' oracle is linear on the number of input qubits n, $\mathcal{O}(n) = \mathcal{O}(\log N)$.

6.3 Empirical Measurement of Circuit Depth

To further reinforce the depth complexity study, an empirical analysis is also presented. In order to do this, we have generated the oracles for different numbers of k, n_k, and n. To properly perform this analysis, before measuring depth, all the circuits have been transpiled using one of the IBM quantum computer backends. In particular, the one used has been *fake_washington_v2*, which has the same properties (gate set, coupling map, etc.) as the real quantum device Washington.[6].

Figure 11 shows the depth of the oracle with respect to the number of input qubits n, for different values of k and n_k. It can be noticed that the depth grows linearly as the number of input qubits increases. This is an expected behaviour as theoretically explained above.

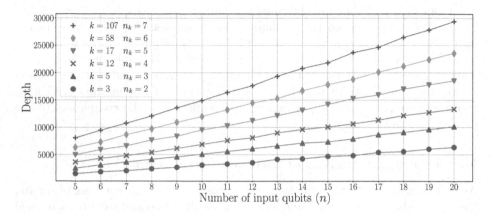

Fig. 11. Depth (y-axis) against number of input qubits n (x-axis) for different values of k.

It can also be noticed that the slope of the graphic grows as the number of qubits in the remainders register n_k increases. This is also an expected behaviour, as the depth of the modulo addition grows linearly with the number of qubits on which it is applied. This behaviour can be observed in Fig. 12. This figure shows the growth of the depth with respect to the number k whose multiples are to be computed. This analysis has been conducted by choosing several pseudo-random numbers in each interval $[2^{n_k-1}, 2^{n_k})$, with $n_k \in \{3, 4, 5, 6, 7\}$. These intervals are delimited by vertical dotted lines on the figure. It can be observed that the depth for each value holds mostly constant in these intervals. This means that the depth increments are mainly caused by the growing number of n_k qubits required to store the remainders of k (largest number stored is $k - 1$).

Lines in both figures are mere visual guides and do not represent any data.

7   Composability and Further Uses

In this section, we show how the proposed oracle can be further reused by providing some examples. First, we showcase how the 'multiples of' oracle can be composed with other oracles. Second, we explain how the oracle can be modified to obtain, instead of multiples of a number k, numbers with a determined

---

[6] https://qiskit.org/documentation/apidoc/providers_fake_provider.html.

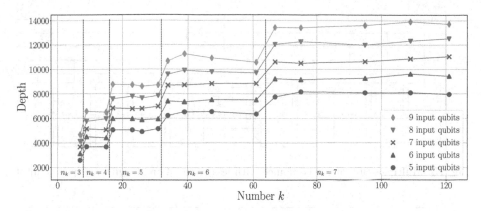

Fig. 12. Depth (y-axis) against k (x-axis) for different amounts of input qubits (n). The corresponding value of n_k for each k is displayed.

remainder when dividing by k. Last, both of these options are combined. Both circuit and results of simulations are displayed in each case. The conditions for the simulations are the same as previously described in Sect. 5.

7.1   Multiples and Less-Than Oracle

We show an example on how to obtain the multiples of a given number k smaller than m. In order to do so, the 'multiples of' oracle and the 'less-than' oracle [20] are composed[7]. However, this composition is not trivial since it must be applied in an specific way. The oracle to compose with ('less-than' in this example) must be applied controlled by the qubits in the remainders register $rq_0, \ldots, rq_{n_k-1}$ and targeted on the input register $q_0, \ldots, q_{n-1}$. This oracle substitutes the multi-controlled Z-gate which is used originally to mark all the multiples.

In this example, the choices are $k = 5$, $m = 14$, $n = 5$. Hence, the desired states are the multiples of 5 smaller than 14 from 0 to 31. The implementation of this oracle can be found in Fig. 13. The results of the simulation using only one repetition of the Grover iterator is in Fig. 14. The results are, as expected, the states amplified of the multiples of 5 less than 14.

7.2   Numbers with Any Remainder

This subsection shows how to change the multiples oracle in order to obtain numbers with any remainder r when dividing by a given integer k. The operation 'multiples of' explained so far is the particular case $r = 0$. In this example, we show the oracle taking $k = 6$, $r = 3$, $n = 5$, formally, $p \equiv 3 \bmod 6$. The oracle can be found in Fig. 15. Notice that, when giving a π-phase with gate CCZ in the remainders register, there are only X gates in the qubit rq_2, hence marking

---

[7] The 'multiples of' oracle can be combined with any other phase-marking oracle.

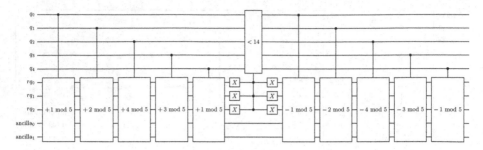

Fig. 13. Multiples of 5 oracle combined with less than 14 oracle with a 5 qubits input.

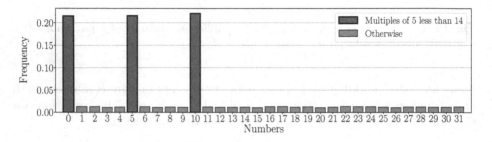

Fig. 14. Results of simulating the circuit of multiples of 5 less than 14 with a 5 qubits input.

those states where $|rq_2\, rq_1\, rq_0\rangle = |011\rangle = |3\rangle = |r\rangle$. The results of the simulation using only one repetition of the Grover iterator is shown in Fig. 16 and match the expected results for this operation.

7.3   Numbers with Any Remainder and Range of Integers

This subsection shows how to combine the oracle of numbers with a determined remainder when dividing by a number and the range of integers oracle presented in [21]. For instance, here we show the oracle for integers $p \equiv 5 \bmod 9$ and $p \in [12, 28]$. The oracle can be found in Fig. 17. Notice that, as in Subsect. 7.1, there is an oracle controlled by the qubits in the remainders register. However, in this case, the X gates are arranged such that the oracle is activated when the qubits in the remainders register are in the state $|rq_3\, rq_2\, rq_1\, rq_0\rangle = |0101\rangle = |5\rangle$. The results of the simulation using only one repetition of the Grover iterator is shown in Fig. 18.

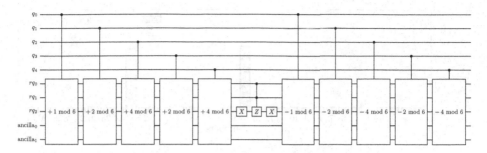

Fig. 15. Numbers $p \equiv 3$ mod 6 oracle with a 5 qubits input.

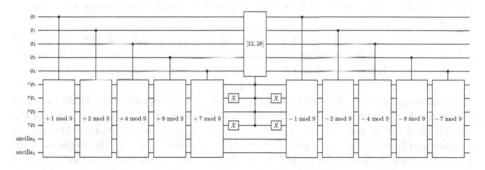

Fig. 16. Results of simulating the circuit of numbers $p \equiv 3$ mod 6 with a 5 qubits input.

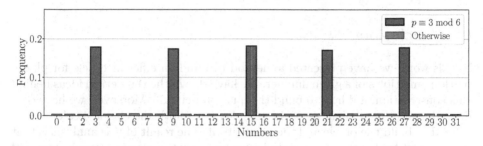

Fig. 17. Numbers $p \equiv 5$ mod 9 with $p \in [12, 28]$ oracle with a 5 qubits input.

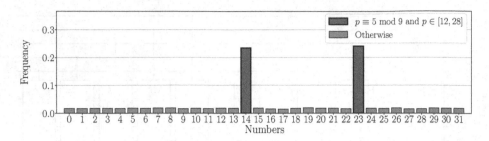

Fig. 18. Results of simulating the circuit of numbers $p \equiv 5 \mod 9$ with $p \in [12, 28]$ with a 5 qubits input.

8   Conclusions

In this work, we have presented a method to build an efficient oracle for phase-marking multiples of a given number. We have shown the theoretical ideas behind this construction and how to build the quantum circuit. Moreover, we have conducted a theoretical analysis of the complexity of both the classical calculations needed to build the oracle and the oracle itself. The result of this analysis is that our method leads to an exponential speedup over the classical one in terms of the required classical computations. Finally, further functionalities are explored. Through examples and simulations we show how to compose the 'multiples of' oracle with other oracles and also how numbers with other properties can be obtained.

This work is one of the steps taken to create an efficient set of tools of quantum software for working with integers. We hope these tools can be reused by quantum software developers to create new quantum algorithms.

Acknowledgements. This work has been financially supported by the Ministry of Economic Affairs and Digital Transformation of the Spanish Government through the QUANTUM ENIA project call - Quantum Spain project, by the Spanish Ministry of Science and Innovation under project PID2021-124054OB-C31, by the Regional Ministry of Economy, Science and Digital Agenda, and the Department of Economy and Infrastructure of the Government of Extremadura under project GR21133, and by the European Union through the Recovery, Transformation and Resilience Plan - NextGenerationEU within the framework of the Digital Spain 2026 Agenda.

We are grateful to COMPUTAEX Foundation for allowing us to use the supercomputing facilities (LUSITANIA II) for calculations.

Repository. The code used for this paper can be found in the following repository: https://github.com/JSRivero/oracle-multiples

Appendix A

Data: Number of powers n and a natural number k
Result: List of remainders r_i of 2^i when divided by k
$\qquad r_i \equiv 2^i \bmod k$ for $i \in [0, n-1]$
list_remainders $\leftarrow list(n)$;
$r \leftarrow 1$;   /* as $2^0 \equiv 1 \bmod k$ for any $k \in \mathbb{N}$ */
for $i = 1$ *to* $n - 1$ **do**
$\quad \mid \quad r' \leftarrow 2 \cdot r$;
$\quad \mid \quad$ **if** $r' < k$ **then**
$\quad \mid \quad \mid \quad r \leftarrow r'$
$\quad \mid \quad$ **else**
$\quad \mid \quad \mid \quad r \leftarrow r' - k$
$\quad \mid \quad$ **end**
$\quad \mid \quad$ list_remainders$[i] \leftarrow r$
end
Algorithm 2: Algorithm for computing the remainders of the first n powers of 2 when divided by k

It can be noticed that this algorithm performs at most 3 operations each iteration, and has n iterations, hence its complexity is $\mathcal{O}(n)$.

References

1. Beauregard, S.: Circuit for shor's algorithm using 2n+3 qubits (2002). https://doi.org/10.48550/ARXIV.QUANT-PH/0205095, https://arxiv.org/abs/quant-ph/0205095
2. Bichsel, B., Baader, M., Gehr, T., Vechev, M.: SILQ: a high-level quantum language with safe uncomputation and intuitive semantics. In: Proceedings of the 41st ACM SIGPLAN Conference on Programming Language Design and Implementation, pp. 286–300. PLDI 2020, Association for Computing Machinery, New York, NY, USA (2020). https://doi.org/10.1145/3385412.3386007
3. Brassard, G., Hoyer, P., Mosca, M., Tapp, A.: Quantum amplitude amplification and estimation. Contemp. Math. **305**, 53–74 (2002)
4. Chivers, I., Sleightholme, J., Chivers, I., Sleightholme, J.: An introduction to algorithms and the big o notation. Introduction to Programming with Fortran: With Coverage of Fortran 90, 95, 2003, 2008 and 77, pp. 359–364 (2015)
5. Classiq: Classiq arithmetic oracle. https://docs.classiq.io/0-13/user-guide/builtin-functions/arithmetic/arithmetic-expression.html
6. Coppersmith, D.: An approximate Fourier transform useful in quantum factoring. arXiv preprint quant-ph/0201067 (2002)
7. Draper, T.G.: Addition on a quantum computer (2000). https://doi.org/10.48550/ARXIV.QUANT-PH/0008033, https://arxiv.org/abs/quant-ph/0008033
8. Green, A.S., Lumsdaine, P.L., Ross, N.J., Selinger, P., Valiron, B.: Quipper: A scalable quantum programming language. SIGPLAN Not. **48**(6), 333–342 (2013). https://doi.org/10.1145/2499370.2462177

9. Grover, L.K.: A fast quantum mechanical algorithm for database search (1996). https://doi.org/10.48550/ARXIV.QUANT-PH/9605043, https://arxiv.org/abs/quant-ph/9605043

10. Grover, L.K.: Quantum computers can search rapidly by using almost any transformation. Phys. Rev. Lett. **80**(19), 4329–4332 (1998). https://doi.org/10.1103/physrevlett.80.4329

11. Harrow, A.W., Hassidim, A., Lloyd, S.: Quantum algorithm for linear systems of equations. Phys. Rev. Lett. **103**, 150502 (2009). https://doi.org/10.1103/PhysRevLett.103.150502, https://link.aps.org/doi/10.1103/PhysRevLett.103.150502

12. Hidary, J.D., Hidary, J.D.: A brief history of quantum computing. Quant. Comput. Appl. Approach. 15–21 (2021)

13. Kay, A.: Tutorial on the quantikz package. arXiv preprint arXiv:1809.03842 (2018)

14. Klappenecker, A., Roetteler, M.: Quantum software reusability. Int. J. Found. Comput. Sci. **14**(05), 777–796 (2003)

15. Leymann, F.: Towards a pattern language for quantum algorithms. In: Feld, S., Linnhoff-Popien, C. (eds.) QTOP 2019. LNCS, vol. 11413, pp. 218–230. Springer, Cham (2019). https://doi.org/10.1007/978-3-030-14082-3_19

16. Montanaro, A.: Quantum algorithms: an overview. npj Quant. Inf. **2**(1), 1–8 (2016)

17. National Academies of Sciences, Engineering, and Medicine and others: Quantum computing: progress and prospects (2019)

18. Nielsen, M.A., Chuang, I.: Quantum computation and quantum information. Phys. Today. **54**, 60 (2002)

19. Preskill, J.: Quantum computing in the NISQ era and beyond. Quantum **2**, 79 (2018)

20. Sanchez-Rivero, J., Talaván, D., Garcia-Alonso, J., Ruiz-Cortés, A., Murillo, J.M.: Automatic generation of an efficient less-than oracle for quantum amplitude amplification (2023). https://doi.org/10.48550/ARXIV.2303.07120, https://arxiv.org/abs/2303.07120

21. Sanchez-Rivero, J., Talaván, D., Garcia-Alonso, J., Ruiz-Cortés, A., Murillo, J.M.: Some initial guidelines for building reusable quantum oracles (2023). https://doi.org/10.48550/arXiv.2303.14959

22. da Silva, A.J., Park, D.K.: Linear-depth quantum circuits for multiqubit controlled gates. Phys. Rev. A. **106**, 042602 (2022). https://doi.org/10.1103/PhysRevA.106.042602, https://link.aps.org/doi/10.1103/PhysRevA.106.042602

23. Qiskit, A., et al.: An open-source framework for quantum computing (2021). https://doi.org/10.5281/zenodo.2573505

24. Zhao, J.: Quantum software engineering: Landscapes and horizons (2021). https://doi.org/10.48550/ARXIV.2007.07047, https://arxiv.org/abs/2007.07047

Orchestrating Information Governance Workloads as Stateful Services Using Kubernetes Operator Framework

Cataldo Mega[✉][iD]

University of Stuttgart, Universitätsstraße 38, 56095 Stuttgart, Germany
cataldo.mega@ipvs.uni-stuttgart.de

Abstract. Regulatory compliance is forcing organizations to implement an information governance (IG) strategy, but many are struggling to evolve their IG solutions due to their legacy architecture, as they are not designed to adapt to new business models and for the growing amount of unstructured data produced by a potentially worldwide audience. One of the biggest problems faced is continuously determining data value and adaptation of measures to keep risks and operational costs under control. One way to solve this issue is to leverage cloud technology and find an affordable approach to migrate legacy solutions to a cloud environment. In most cases, this means de-composing monolithic applications, refactoring components and replacing outdated homegrown deployment technologies with cloud-native, automated deployment and orchestration services. Our goal is to show how operational costs can be reduced by running refactored versions of IG solutions in clouds with a minimum of human intervention. This paper discusses the steps to evolve a legacy multi-tier IG solutions from physical to containerized environments by encapsulating human operator knowledge in cloud topology and orchestration artifacts, with the goal of enabling automated deployment and operation in Kubernetes (K8s) managed execution environments.

Keywords: Information governance · IG workloads · cloud · stateful services

1 Introduction

Every company is subject to three basic business metrics; Value, cost and risk. They form the basis of any Enterprise Information Management (EIM) system. IG adds governance controls to information lifecycles and becomes the control authority for Information Lifecycle Governance (ILG). ILG starts with the creation and extends to the disposition of data. Data sets in the IG context represent governance metadata needed to control how data is processed and to create an appropriate governance context derived from applicable company policies, regulations and standards through the use of Records Lifecycle Management (RLM). This means that governance records relate to the security, classification, retention, and disposition of data. In practical terms, IG consists of implementing an Information Governance Program (IGP) that helps to steer information lifecycles based on actual data value. As a result, ILG workflows through their processes

M. Aiello et al. (Eds.): SummerSOC 2023, CCIS 1847, pp. 125–143, 2023.
https://doi.org/10.1007/978-3-031-45728-9_8

implement three key activities: 1) Use of analytics to determine and maximize data value as context erodes; 2) Enforce archiving of data onto tiered storage to ensure storage cost declines as value declines; 3) Trigger disposal of obsolete data to avoid cost and eliminate risk. As a result, in addition to actual business workloads, these activities also produce typical ILG workloads that an EIM system must handle.

1.1 Problem Statement and Requirements

Today, legacy IG solutions operating in a global open market have to deal with an increasing workload caused by international regulation pushing them to its operational and financial limits. The root cause of these shortcomings is a monolithic solution design and a production system running on a static IT infrastructure. These factors prevent flexibility at component level and elasticity at IT resource level, and are therefore costly to operate and maintain. One way out of this situation is to migrate these solutions to cloud environments and take advantage of the economies of scale where the sharing of IT resources makes it possible to minimize operational costs and optimize resource consumption through automation. Unlike traditional IT systems, clouds automate operational cost control by monitoring key performance indicators that report on cloud resource consumption, and more important make changes to the used infrastructure through dynamic provisioning and de-provisioning requests. This paper proposes steps to evolve and adapt the legacy architecture of IG solutions designed for bare metal production environments to modern cloud environments. To prove the feasibility of our approach, we implemented a prototype of an IG solution running on a Kubernetes-managed (K8s) platform using the operator pattern promoted by the Cloud Native Computing Foundation (CNCF) [1].

1.2 Contributions and Outline of this Paper

Contribution 1: We decomposed our IG solution, reworked its legacy design, and made the necessary changes to automatically deploy and operate it in a K8s execution environment. Major focus has been put into refactoring component and deployment models and the consolidation of the tier-based high availability (HA) design before moving from a bare-metal to a containerized on virtualized deployment model, shown on Fig. 3. Contribution 2: We formalized the knowledge of human operators and implemented a resilient IG solution that models HA, disaster recovery (DR) and scale-out by incorporating infrastructure operational logic into the design and implementation of stateless and stateful cloud services running under the control of the K8s orchestrator.

The remainder of this paper is structured as follows: Sect.: 2 presents a blue-print for IG solutions and an associated component model that we derived from a representative set of IG use cases. Some background on the benefits that the cloud offers for IG workloads is also provided. Section: 3 introduces the fundamental aspects of deployment topologies for IG solutions and discusses traditional versus cloud-native deployment models. It also briefly explains how K8s based workload orchestration works in the cloud. Section: 4 presents our solution approach. Section: 5 introduces the stateful IG solution prototype and its services. Section: 6 details the prototype development and the system under test (SUT) used. Section: 7 discusses the evaluation performed and the test results produced; Sect.: 8 presents our conclusion and provides an outlook on future work.

2   Background

In order to bring together IG solutions and the cloud we need to look at the requirements and workloads that regulations add to typical production systems.

IG requirements are mainly derived from corporate policies, regulations and standards. They influence the solutions design and define RLM control structures required for EIM and RLM lifecycles processes as described by the following use cases (UC) out of the EIM, RLM application domains:

- UC1 (EIM): Collect and classify enterprise data from known sources.
- UC2 (EIM): Load, store, index and secure data in enterprise repositories.
- UC3 (EIM): Search, access and retrieve information from the repositories.
- UC4 (RLM): Apply regulatory security, classification, retention, hold, and disposition policies.
- UC5 (RLM): Support legal cases through e-discover, aggregate and transfer case data on hold.

2.1 ILG Workload Models

By definition, a workload is defined as a representative mix of primitive operations performed against a system. The workloads implied by the UC1 – UC5 use cases fall into the following categories (details are discussed in Mega [5]):

- WL1: This workload is created by interactive users and external agents using web-requests through Https/REST issued against the IG services APIs.
- WL2: Is an interactive- and bulk workload, using lower-level application logic performing database operations consisting of a representative mix of primitive operations like: Create, Retrieve, Update, Delete and Search (CRUDS).
- WL3: Is an interactive- and bulk workloads using low-level file system functions against persisted files, consisting of digital objects of any type, format and size.

Together, use cases, workloads and real-world experience helped define an IG solution and blueprint as shown in Fig. 1 below.

The blueprint consists of seven key solution components, listed as CM1 to CM7.

Going left to right there is: CM1: Aggregates the subcomponents Data Collection, Classification, Assessment and Ingest. CM2: Content Services: Providing Access, Index, Search, Retrieval, Security and Management functions.

CM3: Records Services: These are, Classification, Retention, Disposition and Compliance. CM4: Case Management Services: Consisting of e-Discovery, Legal Data Requests, and Holds. CM5: Content Analytics: Related to, business Classification, Statistics, Reporting. CM6: Repository Services: Provide Information Retrieval, Catalog and Archive functions. CM7: Platform Services: Address Compute, Storage, and Network needs.

For a reference and comparison we looked at architectures published by California Department of Technology [6], Alfresco [7], IBM Cloud Design Center [3], IBM Content Manager Enterprise Edition [4], IBM FileNet Content Manager [8], and other major players in this domain. Workloads, similar to the one defined before, are discussed in Mega [5] and in Lebutsch [9].

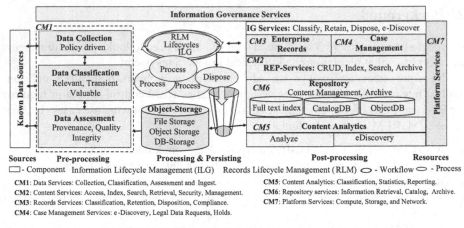

Fig. 1. ILG Solution blueprint and component.

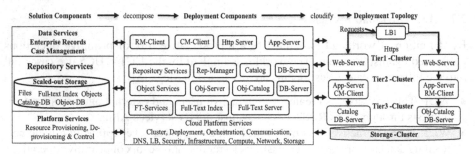

Fig. 2. Steps to create an ILG solution component model and deployment topology.

Both performed similar tests and used a deployment topology similar to that on the far right of Fig. 2. Moving from left to right, we sketched the steps in which the IG solution on the left is broken down into individual, self-sufficient components then assembled into a deployment package along with platform components and arranged as a deployable topology graph using a multi-tier application pattern, shown on the far left.

2.2   The Benefit of Clouds

Today's cloud platforms offer dynamic resource provisioning, scalability and efficiency to applications that are both containerized and virtualized - characteristics that legacy IG solutions lack. Virtualization affects physical production environments; it transforms physical infrastructure into purely virtual infrastructure through a Soft-ware Defined Infrastructure (SDI) approach. Containerization is done at the solution level by breaking down monolithic solutions into independent components that are suitable for running inside containers. Our approach follows the concept of a composable solution that runs on top of a composable infrastructure as coined by Gartner [2]. This approach suggests that IT resources are dynamically allocated through APIs based on policies. Composable in this context means striving for fully automated IT resource lifecycle management, where application workload pattern and Service Level Agreements (SLA) trigger resource provisioning and de-provisioning events. To prove this approach, we implemented a prototype using the IBM Content Services Reference Architecture [3] guidelines and a subset of IBM Content Management [4] family of products.

3 Foundation

Before cloud, there was a gap between cluster and cluster management. The topology graph of Fig. 2 emphasizes this aspect were each tier is designed as a cluster of applications/resources pair configured to address the need for service resiliency and scale using component-specific cluster management logic. IG solutions typically consists of multiple tiers. Examples are a web server tier, an application server tier hosting a content repository for managing unstructured content, a database server tier for storing meta data and a storage tier to persist digital content. Service high availability mandates that every tier withstands component failure therefore a high availability solution requires a high availability configuration for every tier. The complexity of configuring high availability holistically stems from the fact that different tier and server types use different approaches to high availability, consisting of specific operational logic, to holistically maintain a defined application state and meet established service level agreements (SLA). SLAs are measured through key performance indicators like: health (alive, dead), response time and throughput. On clouds, cluster operations are consolidated, centralized and application agnostic. Cloud applications are deployed in container together with their runtime environments, in units called Pod. Pod cluster management is an integral part of the cloud platform and independent of application type. Pods are the smallest deployable units in Kubernetes [10]. Cluster of Pods are centrally managed by the K8s control plane, which acts as a replacement for the legacy, tier-specific cluster management. This feature is the biggest advantage for a traditional multi-tier solution. By migrating legacy applications from bare-metal to the cloud, it is possible to close the gap between clusters and cluster management, simplifying and consolidating the operation of an IG production system.

3.1 Virtualizing and Componentizing a Monolithic IG Solution

Figure 3 is a visual of the platform related migration steps necessary for moving IG solutions from bare metal (left) through virtualization to containerized on virtualized (right) cloud execution environments, as suggested by the CNCF [1].

The refactored IG solution design which we used to develop the prototype required the following migration steps: 1) We decomposed the IG solution design in to smaller independent components; 2) We then virtualized the production environment, selecting OpenStack and KVM as the cloud platform/hypervisor technology (Gang [11]); 3) The third step was to containerize the chosen components using Docker for the container and Kubernetes for the cluster and orchestration technology (Trybek [12], Hagemann [13]) and applied it to the stateless application-tier components; 4) The last step included developing the stateful services based on Kubernetes StatefulSets and the operator framework (Wang [14]). Throughout development our focus was on the re-design but were

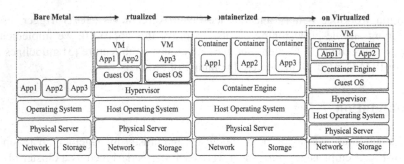

Fig. 3. Migrating from bare metal to containerized on virtualized.

possible also replacement of old components with new cloud-ready technology. As an example, physical components like load balancer (LB), compute server and some networks were replaced with virtual resources provisioned by the cloud platform. Web[1] and application[2] tiers-specific cluster management was replaced with K8s built-in Pod cluster management. Only the management of the database cluster required a custom developed database operator for the DB2 HA-reconciliation and cluster administration logic.

3.2 Comparing Physical vs Virtual Infrastructure Models

Figure 4 shows the deployment topologies of both the original physical production system versus the new virtual, cloud-based production platforms. On the left, you see the legacy system deployed on bare metal servers, in a static, pre-configured production environment. This configuration does not support dynamic topology changes as physical resources are provisioned manually and on request. In these environments software triggered dynamic pro(de)visioning events are not an option. In addition, tier-specific cluster management requires more complex planning and labor intensive operator interventions.

The three clusters (Cluster1–3) on the left of Fig. 4 relate to the three tiers (T1 -T3), web, application and database in a physical environment. The right side shows the same configuration but with a K8s assisted deployment topology optimized for managing the container on virtualized infrastructure. The benefit gained is a consolidated platform built-in cluster management, including a centralized service orchestration facility. In addition, the database specific cluster management is controlled alongside through the K8s APIs using a custom database operator.

---

[1] https://www.ibm.com/docs/en/ibm.

[2] https://www.ibm.com/docs/en/was/9.0.5?topic=websphere-application-server-overview.

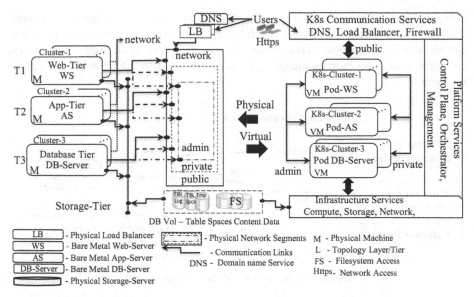

Fig. 4. Migrating solutions from physical to virtual infrastructures.

3.3 Kubernetes Stateful Architecture and its Entities

For a better understanding of our solution approach, we introduce Kubernetes, its components, resources and the operator framework at the high-level. The most important components of K8s are: Controller, Scheduler, Configuration Database (ETCD), a Node (VM), and the actual Operator.

The Deployment, Service and StatefulSets are K8s script resources that are required to define deployment topology and runtime context using YAML grammar.

More specifically their definition is as follows:

- A Deployment is a declarative description of PODs, who carry stateless services.
- A StatefulSets[3] is a declarative description of PODs, carrying stateful services.
- A Service is a declarative way to expose PODs to the external world. The Service defines network access and load-balancing policies to PODs hosting applications that provide the actual service.
- A Custom Resource Definition (CRD) is a declarative description representing a resource known to, but not managed by K8s.
- A Custom Resource (CR) is a component implementing a custom control loop used to manage a custom resource throughout its entire lifecycle. A CR carries the human operator knowledge in form of resource specific implementation artifact.
- An Operator is a K8s extension that allows custom software to be management from within Kubernetes using a Custom Resource Definition (CRD) and the corresponding Custom Resource (CR) component via K8s APIs.

By definition, an IG solution consists of components that provides both stateless and stateful services. This means that the following 3 K8s resources must be used to

---

[3] https://kubernetes.io/docs/concepts/workloads/controllers/statefulset/.

bring stateless and stateful services under the control of K8s: Deployments for stateless services; StatefulSets for modeling stateful services and operators that use application-specific management logic to control topology changes via APIs. Figure 5 shows the control flow of an operator for managing the lifecycle based on state changes of a custom resource.

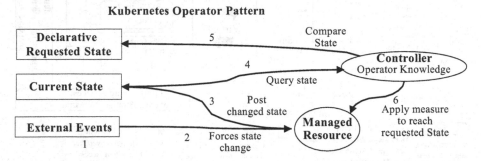

Fig. 5. K8s control loop of the operator pattern.

In summary, Kubernetes manages the execution environment at and above the Pod level, but not the application within the containers. The operator[4] pattern is intended to close this gap. That is, human operator functions were made available to a K8s operator to manage sets of services in an automated way via K8s APIs. For example, the imitation of a human database operator through database-specific administration logic implemented with scripts or program modules that specify setup, configuration and management of the database in a production environment.

4   Solution Approach

For our IG solution design, we envisioned a 2-level hierarchy of five K8s operators. The first operator on the left of Fig. 6 represents the top level ILG service operator, who controls and monitors the four operators at the 2nd-level. These are the Repository service, the Client service, the ObjServer service, and the DB service, which together form the four-tiered deployment topology shown in Fig. 4. As can be seen, the web and application tiers are mapped to three stateless services implemented as K8s Deployments. The combined database and storage tier are implemented through a K8s StatefulSet, which is used to control and manage the DB service operator, as shown in Fig. 6, bottom right. The DB service operator contains the definition of the DB cluster and the logic required to support high availability, read-scalability and disaster recovery. We deployed and tested the prototype implementation in 2 phases. In the first phase, we focused on the stateless services of the web and application tier, which are shown as the upper part of the topology graph in Fig. 7. In the second phase, we developed and deployed the underlying stateful repository services, including the database and storage tiers shown in the image at the bottom of the topology graph.

---

[4] https://kubernetes.io/docs/concepts/workloads/controllers/statefulset/.

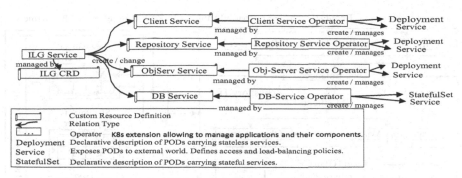

Fig. 6. K8s operator hierarchy for managing ILG deployment topology.

By stateful database services we mean a service that is resilience to component failures. In our context this might be database instance, a storage or a network failure. The implemented solution is a shared-nothing database cluster with at least 3 independent database instances and a mechanism that replicates the database data using synchronous or asynchronous replication.

The rest of this papers focuses on the aspect of highly available stateful database services and the required orchestration logic used, which we derived from database product guidelines and our own expertise.

4.1 K8s Operator Extended Control Loop

To support a stateful database service by running a cluster of database instances in containers on a virtualized in environment, it was necessary to design database-specific cluster management using the components and a topology shown in Fig. 7. The integration of the database cluster and its execution environment is controlled by the StatefulSet complemented by the DB2 operator, together they control the database overall state and topology through the K8s control plane. The DB2 operator and respective custom control loop is shown in the lower left part of Fig. 7. It also shows the K8s and the DB2 control loops, so-called MAPE loops, a concept that is being discussed in Maurer [15]. MAPE stands for Monitor, Analyze, Plan and Execute, basically the chain of processes that, through decision logic determines what activities must follow after a change of the desired state of the stateful service. The MAPE process steps are: Monitor the target resource state; Analyze and compare current state with the desired state; In case of misalignments, Plan what activities to perform; Execute the reconciliation plan, taking the necessary actions to align current state with desired service state.

4.2 Related Work

The prototype implementation work was done in the course of 4 master thesis at the university of Stuttgart by Gang [11], Trybek [12], Hagemann [13] and Wang [14]. The concept design around dynamic topology was published by Mega [5], Börner [16], and contribution on how application might use the MAPE loop concept came from Ritter [17]. A concept model of an ECM system including governance services was provided

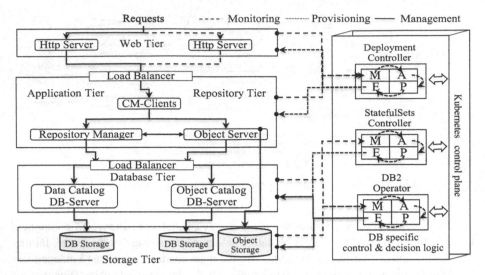

Fig. 7. ILG solution deployment topology and the K8s control loops.

by the IBM Cloud Architecture Center [3]. The CNCF [1] published white paper on the operator pattern provided the ground work for our migration approach. Andrikopoulos [18] in his paper outlines a generic introduction on how to adapt applications for the cloud. Kubernetes best practices, specific to StatefulSets and operators came from Palak [19] at Google, and aspects of EIM practices in companies from Chaki [20]. The California Department of Technology [6] published an ECM reference architecture, that was complemented by information management governance guidelines from Victoria State Government [21] and other agencies, which we used to align our blueprint with. Maurer et al. [15] elaborated on MAPE for autonomic management of cloud infrastructures. Overall, our research lead to several academic sources on stateful services on cloud, but none that address specifically the aspect of refactoring monolithic, legacy IG solutions and none how to move them on cloud execution platforms.

5   The ILG Repository Stateful Service Prototype

Compared to stateless services, stateful services are more complex to design and to implement because K8s was initially designed for stateless services only. Stateful services were introduced later for integrating custom resources. For the prototype we chose an IG solution based on IBM ECM [4] and other necessary components, consisting of IBM Content Navigator, IBM Content Manager, IBM WebSphere Application Server and the IBM DB2 database server. This decision was based on practical experience with these products, in building ECM production systems that provide information governance services. A knowledge we have acquired through several customer projects. The configuration of the prototype is designed to test scale-out, service availability and disaster recovery and was translated into a set of K8s stateful services. The DB2 service operator is used specifically to automate the management of the DB2 database cluster through K8s APIs.

5.1 Kubernetes Stateful Services Cluster Setup

Figure 8 shows the multi-tiered deployment model of the refactored IG solution which uses K8s automated operating concept. This setup, implements the web tier with Docker-compose and focused on the application and database tiers for our HA testing.

The application cluster at Tier-2 is managed by a K8s Deployment artefact not shown in Fig. 8. Instead, the database cluster uses a K8s StatefulSet together with the DB2 operator as Tier-3. The DB2 StatefulSet defines, creates and controls the Pod cluster, which consists of Pod1 - Pod4 running on Node1and Node2. It defines two service entry points SVC-Read/Write and SVC-Read-only, and ensures that the persistent volumes PV1 - PV4 are attached to the Pods. Each Pod consists of one container that hosts one database instance. The StatefulSet also ensures that each Pod has an ordered, stable identity, a unique network identifier and is bound to its persistent volume (PV), surviving deletions and recreations. If a Pod fails or dies, then the StatefulSet control loop will recreate the Pod with exactly the same identity and rebound them to the original PV, ensuring the Pod can access the previously owned database data.

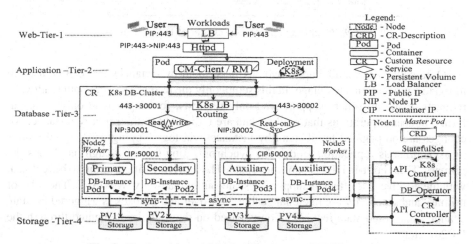

Fig. 8. Deployment model of a K8s cluster of DB2 instances.

The K8s DB2 operator complements the StatefulSet by creating and managing the cluster of DB2 instances using the CRD. The operator itself is deployed in another Pod. Its task is to create the DB2-CR using the DB2-CRD specification, once it is activated. Once active, the Governor, which represents the DB2 cluster control loop, begins monitoring the health of each database instance, continuously compares it to the desired state. If the current state deviates from the desired state, the control loop triggers a series of actions, to reconcile current state with the desired state using database-specific administration logic.

Figure 9 details the DB2 cluster setup in an HA and DR configuration. Primary and secondary instances have each a collocated Governor component.

All four DB-instances have a connection to the DB2 HADR component, which implements the DB2 cluster management logic. Figure 9 also shows the different roles assigned to each cluster members. The primary instance is the cluster leader and owns the reference database. The principal standby instance is attached to the first instance as a peer instance, and its database is the HA-synchronous replication target. Database service fail-over is between primary and standby (the secondary) database instance.

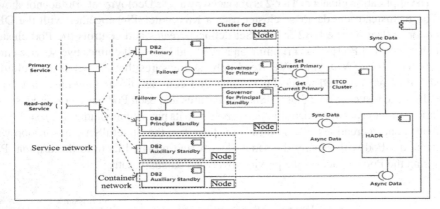

Fig. 9. Component model of a cluster of DB2 instances.

Optionally, there can be up to two auxiliary stand-by instances that can be used to mitigate a production site outage. In this setup, only the primary servers both read/write requests, while all others support read-only requests, forming a read-only scale-out farm. Database operations that modify data are redirected to the primary instance. All changes are propagated to all stand-by instances via log shipping using synchronous or asynchronous replication mode. The synchronization source though, is always the primary. These built-in DB2 capabilities enable HA and DR configurations to be realized, with the positive side effect of supporting scale-out of read-only workloads. The roles of primary and secondary are interchangeable. Fail-over and fallback is triggered by state change events, and state reconciliation is based on the logic implemented through the DB2 operator.

5.2   K8s DB2 Stateful Service Design and Implementation

According to the K8s Operator framework, an operator consists of the following components: API, CRD, CR, a Controller and the resource specific management logic. The operator itself is defined through a K8s 'Deployment' that describes security, roles, accounts management and runs in its own Pod. Figure 10 shows the DB2 operator components and their relationships. By definition, the K8s DB2 operator manages the lifecycle of the DB2 resources, that is, creating and managing the cluster of DB2 database instances that are unknown to K8s and its native cluster management services. In our prototype, the custom resource administration logic is spread among the operator Pod, the DB2 instance Pods and the ETCD Pod. The constituent custom resource components are: Governor, DB cluster controller, DB2 APIs, HADR and ETCD components shown at the bottom of Fig. 10. The ETCD is a distributed key-value store that is used to store the DB-cluster topology information in a look-up table, like: host name, role lock, timestamp and other required configuration parameters.

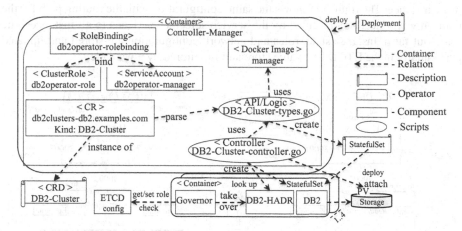

Fig. 10. Components of the Kubernetes Operator for DB2.

The operator component model of Fig. 10 shows the Governor and the HADR component as deployed collocated with the DB instance on every Pod, bottom tight. The DB2 Controller and API, on the other hand, are hosted on the operator Pod, upper part. A possible situation of "split-brain syndrome", i.e. a situation in which both the primary and the secondary instance try to restart at the same time, resulting in duplicate services, is avoided using ETCD as an external reference point monitored by the Governor, as shown on the bottom left in Fig. 10, overseeing the automated fail-over/fallback process. Creating and managing the database topology is done by the DB2 Controller inside the DB2 Operator.

6 DB2-Operator Prototype Test System Setup

We implemented and evaluated the prototype on our department's cloud infrastructure. The test environment consists of OpenStack, which is used to provision compute, storage, network and virtual machines (VM). The VMs run an Ubuntu server, configured with Docker, Compose and Kubernetes. The test infrastructure resources include 3 VMs labeled Node1- Node3, the public and internal networks and 4 physical storage volumes PV1-PV4, as shown in Fig. 11. This setup has one master and two worker K8s nodes. The test system includes: an ETCD cluster, the Google Operator template, the HAProxy load balancer and the DB2 Pod cluster. The actual database instances are loaded into the containers using docker images. The DB2 operator artifacts consist of as set of kubernetes YAML scripts and the custom database cluster management tools, implemented as Python, Go and Bash scripts. Figure 11 shows two aspects of our database test system setup, consisting of four Pods, the test client and the HAProxy used as the load balancer. The database instances are configured to start automatically with the Pod using startup shell scripts that start the DB2 database, the Governor component and the DB2 HADR component. The configuration on the left side of Fig. 11 highlights the routing path for the read/write workload, represented by the service selector leading to the primary instance. The right side shows the same configuration with the routing path for the read-only workload, represented by the service selector that leads to all instances, the scale-out farm. Instance state, roles and network configuration are stored and updated periodically in the ETCD key-value store and monitored by a watchdog.

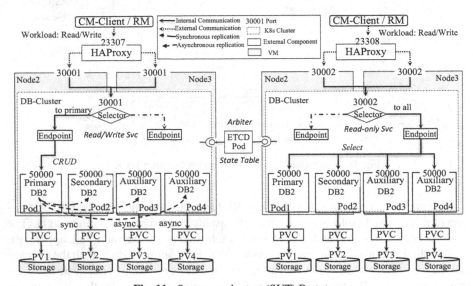

Fig. 11. System under test (SUT) Prototype.

The initialization routines ensure that the K8s service instances receive the correct labels and are associated with corresponding communication endpoints, i.e. their IP addresses and ports. Endpoints configurations are dynamically updated when Pods die or are recreated. Each database instance has a specific role and together represent the DB2 database HA-cluster. Figure 11 also outlines the external and internal communication endpoints and lists the flow of user request for the different workload types.

This test setup includes the HA-Proxy component that plays the role of the request dispatcher and load balancer. We have configured HA-Proxy to run outside of the K8s cluster and to forward incoming client requests to the two worker nodes. HA-Proxy provides a pair of public communications end-points that are linked to the DB service entry points inside the K8s cluster, shown in Fig. 11. K8s Service artifacts act as service proxies of the actual database service. In the case of a read-only workload, the K8s selector (a built-in K8s LB) forwards requests to all Pods across the VM worker nodes to ensure the request traffic is load balanced based on defined policies.

7 Tests, Results and Evaluation

Our test scenarios were created to evaluate the prototype in terms HA, DR and scale-out capabilities. The actual verification tests were developed using a Python client application that simulates an interactive multi-user database transaction workload. We ran several load and scalability tests against the database HA-cluster and collected the results. The external HA-Proxy server provided in-cluster response-time statistics, end-to-end response-times were generated by our own client application. Results include request response times, data throughput, the number of connections, as well as server status, reaction time to failures and service recovery times.

Note: The tests carried out are only indicative and serve to verify the steps of platform migration, estimate approximate effort and prove the feasibility of our approach.

7.1 Service Availability and Failover Scenario

The first test scenario shown in Fig. 12, simulates a failure of the database service by simply deleting the Pod along with the primary database instance, see red lightning bolt at T1. We then measured the time it took until the outage was discovered, the time at which the database service was re-restored and verified the consistency of the database and its data. The relevant HA metrics used are: Reaction time $Trec = T2-T1$; Fail-over time $Tfov = T3-T2$; HA-service restore time $Tha = T4-T3$; and the auxiliary reconfiguration time $Taux = T5-T4$. The sum over the partial times is the overall configuration reset time. Using the interaction diagram of Fig. 12 we have following flow of events: At T1, the Pod of the primary server is deleted and the primary lock (a timestamp) in ETCD is no longer updated. T2 – is the case when the K8s Deployment control loop (C-loop in the diagram) detects that the primary Pod has died, and re-creates the Pod with the same data (PV1) but with new IP address and eventually on a different node; T3 - the Governor on the secondary server detects that the timestamp of the primary lock exceeds the time to live (TTL) and therefore declares it inactive. At this point the secondary takes on the role of the primary. This is done by starting the DB2 HA-specific take-over process and re-establishing the database service.

T4 is when the Governor on the new clone of the old primary Pod through the ETCD database detects that there is a new active primary server and assigns itself the role of the new secondary server, connects as peer, and starts the synchronous database replication. At T5, the two Auxiliary instances become aware of the role change and reconnect to the new primary instance, triggering the database replication, as shown in the interaction diagram of Fig. 12. We performed 10x test runs of the HA failover scenario and measured reaction-, failover- and service recovery times listed in Table 1. The test results are displayed in seconds. The average measured reaction time of the K8s control loop was about ~2 s, while the service recovery time was about ~14 s on average.

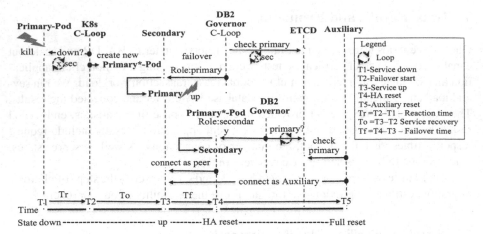

Fig. 12. HA fail-over flow of events and reaction times.

Table 1. DB availability (HA) failover response time test results.

#	Trec (s)	Tfov (s)	Tha (s)
1	2.859	3.621	6.425
2	1.995	4.322	6.839
3	2.403	9.655	18.180
4	2.066	5.856	13.793
5	2.022	36.309	41.639
6	2.051	9.632	14.555
7	1.720	4.839	9.570
8	2.058	29.886	32.728
9	2.624	9.679	18.111
10	2.059	33.286	34.581
Avg.	**2.186**	**14.709**	**19.642**

The variations in failover time, i.e. the time it takes for the new secondary database to restore HA-state, were approximately ~20 s, as this depends on the think time of the governor's control loop, which was configured to 30 s. In the worst case, this means a 30 s wait period before the role change happens, plus some time delay due to system load, which explains the magnitude of the fluctuations in the Tf response time. The results suggest that the reaction time of the K8s control loop is negligible compared to the service recovery time. K8s rebuilds Pods faster than the time it takes for the custom resource takes to restore service. In our test environment, service recovery seems to be in the of range of minutes, while Pod cloning is in the range of tenths of seconds. Overall though, the results obtained prove the feasibility of our approach.

7.2 Read-Only Workload Scalability Test

The first series of tests focuses on determining the response time characteristics of the DB2-cluster under different loads. The test is to create an increasing number of interactive (10–30) virtual users that send a series of SQL requests to a database table that is replicated to the four DB2-cluster members. The workload itself consists of simple select statements that are issued in a loop with a short think time in between. Each run is repeated with 10, 20 and 30 simulated users against 1, then 2, then 3 and finally 4 DB2-instances. Each user sends 1000 requests for a total workload of 10.000, 20.000 and in the third iteration 30.000 read requests, which equates to 30.000 database transactions at peak. Figure 13, shows the response time of Pod/ DB-instances (x-axis) and workloads (colored horizontal lines).

SQL Read Requests (RR) by Concurrent Users (CU)

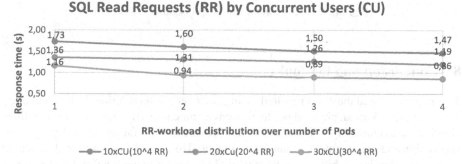

Fig. 13. Average read response time by number of users and DB-instances. (Color figure online)

As can be seen, the three response time graphs all show that time gradually decreases as Pods (instances) are added independent of the workload used: blue (10.000), orange (20.000), grey (30.000). This is Easily explainable, because the workload is distributed across all available instances. Instead, with a constant number of Pods, the response time increases as the workload increases demonstrating the scale-out behavior of the system.

In the second scenario, load balancing across the DB2-cluster is evaluated. With this test case, we investigated the distribution of work among the cluster members by constant load. The results of the three set of tests are shown in Fig. 14. The vertical axis shows the number of read requests generated by the virtual users in batches of 10.000, 20.000 and 30.000 transactions. For each batch, we repeated the test with 1,2,3 and 4 DB2-instances.

The graph shows the system load as color-coded sections of the vertical bars. The blue area represents the primary, brown the secondary, grey the auxiliary-1 and yellow the auxiliary-2 database instance. The number of transactions served by each DB2-instance is proportional to the size of the section in the respective bar.

The result demonstrates, that using a constant workload with a growing number of DB2-instances, the individual load on each instance decreases as the overall workload is distributed across all cluster members.

Here, too, the test results confirm our claim. Therefore, migrating legacy IG solutions to cloud execution environments is feasibility and with an affordable effort. Typical IG solution capabilities such as HA, DR and scale-out are retained, benefiting automated service delivery, flexible resource allocation, and reduced operational costs.

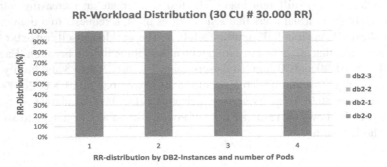

Fig. 14. Read-only workload. Response time and request

8 Conclusion and Outlooks

This paper explored the effort required to migrate a legacy IG solution designed to operate in a pre-configured, physical production environment to a dynamic software-defined cloud infrastructure (SDI). The focus of this work was on refactoring the legacy solution design and successfully moving from a physical to a cloud environment. The benefit gained from this is the ability to orchestrate ILG workloads using stateful services in K8s managed clusters. We have learned that cloud platforms provide cluster control mechanisms and resource topology management across all solution tiers, which can simplify and reduce the application-specific cluster management complexity. With Pod clusters managed by K8s, Pod, Node, Network and Storage management is kept out of application responsibility and centrally consolidated in the cloud platform. This makes application layer-specific cluster management obsolete and solution design leaner. In addition, built-in control loops with the cloud platform enables monitoring of resource health and automatic triggering of provisioning and de-provisioning requests. Component specific lifecycle management tasks are integrated as K8s extensions using the operator pattern. Operators make it possible to take advantage of the elasticity of the cloud infrastructure and react dynamically to changes in workload. The resulting effects are the avoidance of manual interventions, gain in flexibility and the reduction of associated operating costs.

Our prototype leveraged the IBM ECM product stack, consisting of IBM Content Navigator, IBM Content Manager Enterprise Edition, along with the required IBM Web-Sphere Application Server and IBM DB2 database server. We have developed an IG solution design as used by traditional ECM customers world-wide, most of whom still run their systems on-premise on a physical infrastructure. Currently, all products support virtualized environments, but not all support containerized in virtualized environments. We couldn't, find a customer story that holistically shows the migration of an IG solution from physical to cloud, but several blogs explaining cloud implementations of individual component. Future work could focus on real-world production deployments and repeat our tests with more realistic workloads and database sizes.

References

1. CNCF, CNCF operator white paper. https://github.com/cncf/tag-app-delivery/blob/main/operator-wg/whitepaper/Operator-WhitePaper_v1-0.md. Accessed 30 July 2023
2. Panetta, K.: Gartner keynote: the future of business is composable the future of business is composable, 19 October 2020 https://www.gartner.com/smarterwithgartner/gartner-keynote-the-future-of-business-is-composable. Accessed 30 July 2023
3. IBM, Content management: content services reference architecture. https://www.ibm.com/cloud/architecture/architectures/contentManagementdomain/reference-architecture/. Accessed1 Mar 2023
4. IBM Corporation, "IBM Content Manager Enterprise Edition components," IBM Corporation, Online (2023)
5. Mega, C., Waizenegger, T., Lebutsch, D., Schleipen, S., Barney, J.M.: Dynamic cloud service topology adaption for minimizing resources while meeting performance goals. IBM J. Res. Dev. **58**, 1–10 (2014)
6. California department of technology , enterprise content management reference architecture, California department of technology 1325 J Street, Suite 1600, Sacramento, CA 95814 (2014)
7. Alfresco, Alfresco Content Services (2021). https://www.alfresco.com/platform
8. IBM Corporation, "FileNet P8 baseline architecture," IBM Corporation, Online (2023)
9. Lebutsch, D., Bolik, C., Hennecke, M.: Content management as a service—financial archive cloud. Datenbank-Spektrum **10**, 131–142 (2010)
10. kubernetes.io, "Kubernetes Concepts," 30 July 2023. https://kubernetes.io/docs/concepts/. Accessed 30 July 2023
11. Shao, G.: About the design changes required for enabling ECM systems to exploit cloud technology (2020)
12. Trybek, C.: Investigating the orchestration of containerized enterprise content management worklaods in cloud environments using open source cloud technology based on kubernets and docker (2021)
13. Hagemann, P.: About the design changes required for enabling ECM systems to exploit cloud technology (2021)
14. Wang, X.: Orchestrating stateful database services in cloud environments using Kubernetes stateful services framework, OPUS - publication server of the University of Stuttgart (2022)
15. Maurer, M., Breskovic, I., Emeakaroha, V.C., Brandic, I.: Revealing the MAPE loop for the autonomic management of Cloud infrastructures. In: 2011 IEEE Symposium on Computers and Communications (ISCC) (2011)
16. Andreas, B.: Orchestration and provisioning of dynamic system topologies, Stuttgart (2011)
17. Ritter, T., Mitschang, B., Mega, C.: Dynamic provisioning of system topologies in the cloud. In: Enterprise Interoperability V, London (2012)
18. Andrikopoulos, V., Binz, T., Leymann, F., Strauch, S.: How to adapt applications for the cloud environment – challenges and solutions in migrating applications to the cloud. Computing **95**, 493–535 (2013)
19. Bhatia, P., Tee, J.X.: Best practices for building Kubernetes Operators and stateful apps. https://cloud.google.com/blog/products/containers-kubernetes/best-practices-for-building-kubernetes-operators-and-stateful-apps. Accessed 20 October 2018
20. Chaki, S.: Enterprise information management in practice (2015)
21. .StateGovernmentofVictoria, "Information Management Maturity Measurement" (2019)
22. IBM Corporation, "IBM Enterprise Content Management Performance Methodology," IBM Corporation, Online (2015)
23. IBM Corporation, "IBM FileNet Content Manager 5.2High Volume Scalability," IBM SWG, Online (2014)
24. IBM Corporation, "IBM Content Services," IBM Corporation, Online (2022)

Towards Serverless Data Exchange Within Federations

Boris Sedlak[1]([⊠])(iD), Victor Casamayor Pujol[1](iD), Praveen Kumar Donta[1](iD),
Sebastian Werner[2](iD), Karl Wolf[2](iD), Matteo Falconi[3], Frank Pallas[2](iD),
Schahram Dustdar[1](iD), Stefan Tai[2], and Pierluigi Plebani[3](iD)

[1] Distributed Systems Group, TU Wien, 1040 Vienna, Austria
{b.sedlak,v.casamayor,pdonta,dustdar}@dsg.tuwien.ac.at
[2] Information Systems Engineering, Technische Universität Berlin, Berlin, Germany
{sw,kw,fp,st}@ise.tu-berlin.de
[3] Politecnico di Milano, Milan, Italy
{matteo.falconi,pierluigi.plebani}@polimi.it

Abstract. In this paper, we propose a novel approach for sharing
privacy-sensitive data across federations of independent organizations,
taking particular regard to flexibility and efficiency. Our approach benefits from data meshes and serverless computing – such as flexible ad-
hoc composability or minimal operational overheads – to streamline data
sharing phases, and to effectively and flexibly address the specific requirements of highly variable data sharing constellations.

Based on a realistic scenario of data sharing for medical studies in a
federation of hospitals, we propose a five-phase data product lifecycle and
identify the challenges that each phase poses. On this basis, we delineate
how our approach of *serverless data exchange* addresses the identified
challenges. In particular, we argue that serverless data exchange facilitates low-friction data sharing processes through easily usable, customiz-
able, and composable functions. In addition, the serverless paradigm provides high scalability while avoiding baseline costs in non-usage times.
Altogether, we thus argue that the *serverless data exchange* paradigm
perfectly fits federated data sharing platforms.

Keywords: Data Exchange · Data Mesh · Serverless Computation

1 Introduction

Data are one of the most valuable assets in many organizations, equally driving business processes and machine learning algorithms. To further exploit its
potential value, data can be combined and extended with assets that are shared

Funded by the European Union (TEADAL, 101070186). Views and opinions
expressed are however those of the author(s) only and do not necessarily
reflect those of the European Union. Neither the European Union nor the
granting authority can be held responsible for them.

between organizations, rather than sinking into the oblivion of data silos. This is motivated by data as a commodity, generating revenue, or from a research perspective, sharing data within a federation on a give-and-take basis. However, data often contains confidential business insights or personal information; thus the effort to share the data in a secure, trusted, performant, and efficient way – avoiding, for instance, accidental data leaks – becomes crucial. At the same time, the way in which data is needed depends on the *data consumer*. This usually leads to the creation of several copies of the initial dataset, each tailored to a specific consumer. All of these aspects contribute to additional *friction in data management* that in many cases hampers, if not blocks, data sharing [2,7]. We argue that the solution must be aware of these frictions and address most of them through careful distribution of responsibilities among actors [4] and applications. Moreover, we argue that a *federated data exchange platform* can leverage federated resources not only to reduce friction but also to improve performance, energy consumption, and transparency.

This paper introduces a novel data exchange architecture that combines serverless computing advantages with principles of the data mesh [6]. Additionally, we propose a novel data sharing lifecycle and address the critical responsibilities and challenges within these novel federated data exchange platforms. Lastly, we pinpoint the prospect of leveraging serverless data exchange to minimize friction and unlock optimization potential within the federated context.

In the remainder of this paper, we present a motivating scenario from the medical sector in Sect. 2, a data sharing lifecycle in Sect. 3, including responsibilities and challenges of data exchange in federations, and in Sect. 4 introduce our proposed serverless data exchange architecture. Finally, in Sect. 5, we summarize this paper and identify potential future work.

2   Motivating Scenario

The analysis of large and diverse patient datasets is essential for the successful implementation of medical trials; however, this only becomes possible through the aggregation of various sources. In this context, the current challenge is to simplify the data exchange among hospitals, which requires a lot of effort in selecting and preparing the data in compliance with internal regulations and general norms (e.g., GDPR), common data formats (e.g., OMOP), as well as agreements on semantics (e.g., SNOMED).

Based on what is already happening in this community, federations recognizing the importance of data sharing to the advancement of medical studies are under establishment (e.g., Elixir[1]). This association, led by domain experts, would share and enforce an agreement on data discovery, metadata standards, and access functions, and partially automate the enactment of data access policies. From a researcher's perspective, this simplifies the search for data that meet the medical study's requirements and allows quick assembly of large pools of diverse patient data. Nevertheless, additional aspects contribute to the friction

---

[1] https://elixir-europe.org.

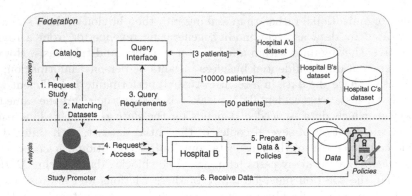

Fig. 1. Study Promoter Workflow

when sharing data and the scenario reported in Fig. 1 helps to describe them. In particular, we visualize the two phases required to enable a joint study in this type of federation: *discovery*, i.e., the search for relevant patient datasets, and the *analysis* of actual data.

To find relevant data, (1) the federation's data catalog (as established in data mesh [6]) provides the ability to search through datasets by filtering based on metadata (e.g., data types, usage consent). The study promoter can use the catalog (2) to find datasets that match their requirements, e.g., patients with a certain pathology or within an age range. The catalog can further (3) provide the number of accessible patients in desired datasets, for example, by querying how many patients consented to the study's purpose. This provides the promoter with a means of selecting the most favorable data providers to enter into an agreement with. After deciding which dataset to use, the analysis phase begins.

Before the data can be accessed directly, (4-5) an agreement must be reached between the study promoter and the data provider(s) to determine the rules for using and accessing the data. As soon as the promoter reaches an agreement with the organizations that offer the fitting datasets, the promoter can request the actual data. First, the provider has to establish *access policies* to ensure that only data that is relevant and contained within the agreement is exposed. Then, *transformations* imposed by the agreement must be performed to ensure interoperability between formats (e.g., unstructured historical patient data, MRI imagery), fulfillment of legal obligations, and compliance with federation guidelines. Both the location of transformations and computations (e.g., analysis steps) must be chosen to ensure compliance with regard to privacy, performance, and sustainable use of the federation's resources. Aggregated and transformed data from different sources in the federation can, in turn, themselves become data sources for other members of the federation if properly accompanied by a set of metadata and policies, and if permitted by the agreement with the original data providers. This allows federation members to reuse and enhance data products without wasting resources by re-performing expensive transformations.

3   Federated Data Product Lifecycle

In data mesh [6], a data product is defined as the smallest unit of architecture. Depending on the data product's domain, a specific team is in charge of managing its lifecycle. Revising this definition in a federated setting, we propose a *federated data product* as the shareable and comparable unit. It is built, according to the service orientation principles, by the data provider and, through the associated API that mediates the access, the data consumer (i.e., the study promoter in Fig. 1) can obtain the data and can combine it with other accessed data products. On this basis, it is also fundamental to define the lifecycle of the federated data products, to offer a systematic and holistic approach to address organizational and technical hurdles (i.e., friction) in exchanging data across organizations by identifying responsibilities, objectives, and design requirements in each phase of a federated data product, akin to the data mesh lifecycle [3].

The lifecycle that we envision is divided into five phases. In the following, we describe each phase and extract *responsibilities* and *challenges* (see Table 1) that a federated sharing platform must address to enable data sharing. Here, we assume the data provider has already joined the federation, including the necessary processes for interacting with other users.

Data Onboarding: Within the first phase of a federated data product lifecycle, data collected by the data provider is *prepared for storage and sharing*. This includes the *data classification*, the setup of necessary *ingestion* – either a one-off transfer or a streaming setup – including necessary transformations, and the *assignment of storage policies*. Once the domain experts have assembled the data, they need to *specify the data product's metadata* in accordance with the federation's metadata model. To ensure that operations on the data comply with internal rules, respective *policies are attached* (e.g., security, confidentiality or access policies or policies that require more complex data transformations to be performed) and provided alongside the metadata. The federated data product is considered onboarded once it is properly described, typically using a domain-specific language [6], and an initial version of it is placed in storage in line with its attached storage policies, e.g., within the EU, using a minimum redundancy, or a given level of encryption.

Publishing: Once the federated data product is onboarded, it can be made available to the federation by *publishing it to a shared data catalog*. This catalog of federated data products must allow consumers to discover data that match their requirements through its metadata. To avoid inconsistencies, the catalog must reflect the latest status of federated data products, e.g., their availability and assigned policies. Additionally, the metadata (e.g., the number of available records) may vary in-between potential consumers based on their identity and access context; these constraints must be reflected through consumer-aware policies. This entails that the metadata provided during the onboarding phase might be enriched further. As part of this phase, domain experts can specify the *capabilities necessary to consume the federated data product*, e.g., the required resources or required product policies enforcement tools.

Table 1. Summary of the challenges for a federated data exchange platform

ID	Challenge	Description	Lifecycle phase
C1	*Shared metadata model*	A domain-specific metadata model to aid the discovery and matching of federated data products	Onboarding
C2	*Policy language*	Usage of a sophisticated policy language to enable platform-supported lawful and trustworthy data exchange	
C3	*Data control plane*	A control plane enabling domain experts to specify and update policies as data changes	
C4	*Stretched data lake*	A policy-based data placement approach utilizing storage and streaming across federated resources	
C5	*Federated data catalog*	Ensure that all members of the federation can discover all federated data products	Publishing
C6	*Consistent metadata*	Keeping browsable metadata (e.g., policies, number of records) in sync with the federated data product	
C7	*Matchmaking*	Support the aligning and matching of consumer requirements to product metadata	
C8	*Context-aware discovery*	Support interactive negotiation queries for consumer-specific metadata, based on product policies, consumer's access purpose, and context	
C9	*Consumer transformations*	Support required consumer transformations, e.g., ensuring format capabilities, storage policy needs	
C10	*Shared agreements*	Ensure that agreements are available in a standardized and immutable format	Sharing
C11	*Enforceable agreements*	Support codifying agreement policies in an unequivocal, automatically enforceable way	
C12	*Trust mechanisms*	Ensure or prove bilateral compliance with accepted agreements (e.g., monetary incentives [8] or trustworthy transformations [5])	
C13	*Data lineage*	Enforcing and capturing agreed-upon consumption contexts, purposes, and transformations	Consumption
C14	*On-demand transformations*	Support smart and on-demand transformations to comply with policies, i.e., allocation of computations within the federation	
C15	*Federated access control*	Support fitting access control mechanisms, compatible with policies and execution environments	
C16	*Enforceable deletions*	Support the deletion of all copies of a federated data product, possibly including derivatives	Discontinue
C17	*Observable lifecycle actions*	Support the audit of all data consumption actions to find and discontinue a federated data product	
C18	*Maintain knowledge*	Preserve functions and system optimization for future improvement	

Sharing: Once the federated data product is published, interested members of the federation can request the data. This is the first occasion where data providers and consumers need to interact. Consumption of federated data products can be bound to various terms and conditions and implies that *both parties come to an agreement* on how the data can be consumed. Agreements *restrict the consumption in various dimensions*, e.g., by posing an end date, stating the purpose of the data consumption, or including transformations that the data must undergo. These transformations can range from projection and selection mechanisms to advanced analysis and are *defined by domain experts*. Thus, agreements are a central part of the sharing processes and govern the rights, responsibilities, and obligations (e.g., technical or legal) of both parties. The agreement is typically formalized in a contract that both *parties sign*, a process that the federated sharing platform must support. From this agreement, the platform can derive the policies that must be enforced, e.g., setting up an access control and/or transformation mechanism or a shared identity provider.

Consumption: Ultimately, the dataset is consumed according to the conditions that were formalized; *compulsory operations (obligations)* included in the agreement must be performed by the federated sharing platform. To support audit mechanisms, *all interactions with the dataset must be documented*, which also improves data lineage, i.e., provide information on how the original data had been altered. At the same time, access logs must comply with privacy guidelines themselves. Moreover, the federated sharing platform can ease the consumption of federated data products, e.g., by *providing means to filter the data*, move it to a different location or *perform a purpose-based transformation* to ensure compliant consumption [9]. We assume that the *data consumer can initiate the consumption* as needed after a sharing agreement is reached. The consumption can be continuous, intermittent, or a one-time event. Thus, the federated sharing platform must support on-demand, continuous, and bulk transformations.

Discontinue: Once the federated data product is no longer needed, or the data provider decides to no longer provide it, it can be discontinued. This phase is the last in the lifecycle and is the counterpart to the onboarding phase. Here, *all active sharing agreements are terminated* and the data product is removed from the catalog. This process may require *prior notification to the data consumers*, e.g., to allow them to adjust their applications or to ensure that they can remove all copies of the federated data product. Here, the *federated control plane* should provide the functionality to ensure that the federated data product is removed from all controlled locations where it was stored, e.g., by allowing an audit of data consumption logs or by providing a means to remove all copies of the federated data product across the shared environment. However, additional nontechnical means such as legal agreements should be in place to ensure compliance.

4   Serverless Data Exchange

This section presents a novel architecture to exchange data products in a federation between organizations while addressing the challenges in Table 1. We leverage properties of serverless computing to enable trustworthy data sharing with minimal operational overhead [10], establishing the concept of serverless data as the capacity to manage the data lifecycle. Figure 2 depicts the serverless architecture we propose as a backbone for the federated sharing platform, following the presented lifecycle phases of a data product. This outlines an initial proposal; however, we are aware that implementing this architecture presents further technical challenges not covered here.

Data Onboarding: Whenever a data provider (e.g., a hospital) offers data products to other members of the federation, the architecture for serverless data exchange provides capabilities to integrate data as a single logical product, regardless of physical (distributed) storage. Policies, supplied by domain experts (**C3**), can be attached to the federated data product before it is exposed through the catalog. Consider that most of the policies at the onboarding phase concern the storage, e.g., where within the federation the product may be stored. Given that policies also depend on the data consumer, the architecture provides

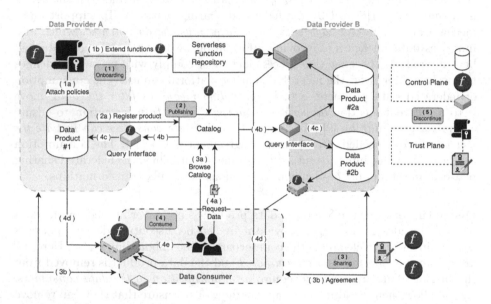

Fig. 2. Serverless data exchange within a federation. *Data Product #1* is onboarded using storage provisioned by the Control plane. Domain Experts supply metadata and policies (1a) which are attached to the federated data product; this might include serverless functions new to the federation that extend the existing function repository (1b). *Data Product #1* is registered by its provider through the federation-wide data catalog (2a), including mandatory policies and functions. The consumer, who is also part of the federation, uses the catalog to browse registered data products (3a) that can be matched to his/her requirements. The consumer then establishes an agreement with both providers (3b) on how data are delivered, i.e., formats, how and where data are transformed according to policies, retention period at the consumer, etc. The consumer requests the data through the catalog by providing the agreement (4a), which is received by the providers' Query Interface (QI) (4b). The QI then instructs individual data products to provide the data to the consumer (4c). Processing of data according to serverless functions can occur at various locations, e.g., at premises provided by the providers or the consumer, or at ad-hoc nodes on any site provided by the Control plane (4d). Finally, the consumer is served the data (4e) as specified in the agreement.

capacities to attach further policies at the following stages. In general, policies might contain references to functions (**C2**) that already exist in the federation; nevertheless, ad-hoc functions can be supplied by federation members.

Publishing: The federated data product is published by its provider using a federation-wide catalog (**C5**), which logically acts as a unified entity for the entire federation. However, the catalog's implementation can be distributed in the federation (e.g., a distributed database (**C6**)); custom instances can be ready on-demand thanks to the serverless functions available at the federation. The catalog includes references to federated data products and their metadata (**C1**), including all policies attached up to that moment. The purpose of the catalog is to make federated data products discoverable in the federation, allowing each member to search the catalog for products that meet their requirements (**C7-8**).

Sharing: When federated data products match the requirements of a consumer (e.g., study promoter), during the sharing phase, all concerned parties need to agree on how data will be provided. Policies specific to the agreement can be supplied, which can either originate from the federation's function repository (**C11**), be incorporated by agreement members, or be provided by third-party entities. All in all, the architecture provides an *extendable and composable framework* that may include any type of function within the agreement. Agreement members (or rather their domain experts) can customize functions by supplying individual implementations or creating multiple versions of functions. These functions can be composed to generate serverless data processing pipelines [10] (**C9**) that transparently manage the transfer of federated data products and conversion from the provider to the consumer. Agreements themselves are stored by all concerned parties (**C10**) and serve as proof of trust between them (**C12**); in this regard, the architecture envisions a Trust plane that ensures proper agreement compliance.

Consumption: The separation of invocation from execution given by the serverless paradigm enables the data provider and consumer to have an execution tailored to their needs. The execution of functions can be optimized by the architecture's Control plane using the computing continuum [1] of the federation (**C4**), e.g., to minimize resource usage or energy consumption. The proposed approach for serverless data facilitates on-demand access to federated data products; hence, functions are created, provisioned, and executed by triggering consumption events (**C14**). Afterward, they are evicted and the federation infrastructure is freed thanks to the scale-to-0 capability of serverless computing. The Trust plane has observability over data transformations, providing data lineage awareness (**C13**) and access control mechanisms (**C15**). Federation members can access published data products according to agreements, i.e., consumers provide a copy of an agreement and identity, which determines how data are prepared and served.

Discontinue: When the agreement finishes (e.g., maximum number of access or time exceeded) or one of the parties withdraws from the agreement, data are no more available. As a consequence, all resources utilized for consumption are released by the Control plane (**C16**); this includes all processing facilities to run serverless functions and consolidated storage for optimizing data consumption. The Control plane will leverage data lineage capabilities from the Trust plane to find all elements that must be discontinued (**C17**). Interestingly, all of the serverless functions in use, as well as Control plane optimization decisions, are kept within the federation for future use and continuous improvement (**C18**).

By seamlessly integrating serverless capabilities with federated data products, we aim to alleviate the provisioning burden of the data provider and eliminate obstacles that impede the exchange of data products, such as the discussed challenges. This relies heavily on components such as the Control plane and Trust plane, which provide resources and establish trust between the parties.

5 Conclusion and Future Work

We proposed a federated data platform that combines serverless computing and data mesh to reduce friction in data exchange across organizational boundaries, such as sharing medical research data. We delineated a five-step data product lifecycle, identified the associated technical challenges, and sketched an overall architecture to address them. Our argument is that through *serverless data exchange*, domain experts can handle complex data behavior, even for ad-hoc and non-continuous data sharing scenarios. Serverless principles support this by providing scalability, flexible placement, and composability of functions.

Having established the conceptual foundations, future work comprises the prototypical implementation and use case-driven evaluation of the platform and its components. This includes aspects such as the allocation of serverless functionality along the compute continuum, consideration of trust-related issues, and questions of overall platform management and control across the federation.

Despite the conceptual nature of considerations presented, we see strong points for *serverless data exchange* to gain significant momentum. Our five-phase data product lifecycle, our identified technical challenges, and our serverless data exchange architecture shall guide and drive respective future activities.

References

1. Dustdar, S., Pujol, V.C., Donta, P.K.: On distributed computing continuum systems. IEEE Trans. Knowl. Data Eng. **35**(4), 4092–4105 (2023). https://doi.org/10.1109/TKDE.2022.3142856
2. Edwards, P., et al.: Science friction: data, metadata, and collaboration. Soc. Stud. Sci. **41**, 667–90 (2011). https://doi.org/10.2307/41301955
3. Eichler, R., et al.: From data asset to data product - the role of the data provider in the enterprise data marketplace. In: Service-Oriented Computing, pp. 119–138 (2022). https://doi.org/10.1007/978-3-031-18304-1_7

4. Eschenfelder, K.R., Shankar, K.: Of seamlessness and frictions: transborder data flows of European and US social science data. In: Sundqvist, A., Berget, G., Nolin, J., Skjerdingstad, K.I. (eds.) iConference 2020. LNCS, vol. 12051, pp. 695–702. Springer, Cham (2020). https://doi.org/10.1007/978-3-030-43687-2_59
5. Heiss, J., Busse, A., Tai, S.: Trustworthy pre-processing of sensor data in data on-chaining workflows for blockchain-based IoT applications. In: Hacid, H., Kao, O., Mecella, M., Moha, N., Paik, H. (eds.) ICSOC 2021. LNCS, vol. 13121, pp. 133–149. Springer, Cham (2021). https://doi.org/10.1007/978-3-030-91431-8_9
6. Machado, I.A., Costa, C., Santos, M.Y.: Data mesh: concepts and principles of a paradigm shift in data architectures. Procedia Comput. Sci. **196**, 263–271 (2022)
7. Sedlak, B., Casamayor Pujol, V., Donta, P.K., Dustdar, S.: Controlling data gravity and data friction: from metrics to multidimensional elasticity strategies. In: IEEE SSE 2023. IEEE, Chicago (2023). (Accepted)
8. Sober, M., et al.: A blockchain-based IoT data marketplace. Cluster Comput., 1–23 (2022). https://doi.org/10.1007/s10586-022-03745-6
9. Ulbricht, M.R., Pallas, F.: CoMaFeDS: consent management for federated data sources. In: 2016 IEEE International Conference on Cloud Engineering Workshop (IC2EW), pp. 106–111 (2016). https://doi.org/10.1109/IC2EW.2016.30
10. Werner, S., Tai, S.: Application-platform co-design for serverless data processing. In: Hacid, H., Kao, O., Mecella, M., Moha, N., Paik, H. (eds.) ICSOC 2021. LNCS, vol. 13121, pp. 627–640. Springer, Cham (2021). https://doi.org/10.1007/978-3-030-91431-8_39

Author Index

M. Aiello et al. (Eds.): SummerSOC 2023, CCIS 1847, p. 155, 2023.
https://doi.org/10.1007/978-3-031-45728-9

Printed in the United States
by Baker & Taylor Publisher Services